The French Connection

The French Connection

Betty Lou Phillips

Gibbs Smith, Publisher
Salt Lake City

First Edition
09 08 07 06 05 10 9 8 7 6 5 4 3 2 1

Published by
Gibbs Smith, Publisher
PO Box 667
Layton, UT 84041

For orders: 1.800.748.5439
www.gibbs-smith.com

Design by Cherie Hanson
Printed and bound in Hong Kong

Library of Congress Cataloging-in-Publication Data

Phillips, Betty Lou.
  The French connection / Betty Lou Phillips.—1st ed.
      p. cm.
  ISBN 1-58685-529-8
  1. Interior decoration--United States—History—21st century. 2.Decoration and ornament—France—Influence. I. Title.

NK2004.15.P55 2005
747'.0973—dc22

2005020807

ON THE FRONT JACKET: *Serenity is a permanent houseguest in a sitting room with pale lavender walls. Antique Swedish chairs surround an eighteenth-century Italianate table. Statue de la Vierge III, an oil on canvas, is by Japanese artist Masao Haijima (1949–), who studied at École des Beaux-Arts, Paris's prestigious national art school on the rue Bonaparte, and now lives in the French capital. The Pan American Art Gallery in Dallas represents him.*

ON THE BACK JACKET: *A silk taffeta from Cowtan & Tout brings streamlined glamour to the guest room whose sitting room is featured on the cover, the title page, and pages 92–93. Gingham became popular in the nineteenth century. Custom side tables wear Ralph Lauren fabric.*

ON THE END PAPERS: *Silk-screened, heat-set châteaux tiles—on tumbled botticino stone—from All Tiled Up in Granada Hills, California, are available through Architectural Design Resources, Houston.*

ON THE TITLE PAGE: *On the opposite side of the sitting room seen on the cover, subtle lavender walls paired with spare furnishings convey a tranquil tone, while white adds crisp definition. Paysage de la Sainte Chapelle #2, an oil on canvas, is by Masao Haijima, whose studio on the majestic avenue de l'Opéra overlooks some of the French capital's most famous rooftops, including Nôtre-Dame and the Louvre.*

OPPOSITE THE COPYRIGHT PAGE: *Not all that glitters is gold. A gourmet kitchen gleams, thanks to a Garland commercial stove, cabinet doors wrapped in stainless steel, and Carrera slab countertops quarried in Italy. Until the end of World War II, bread was mostly round—a shape called a boule. Thus the French word boulangerie, a place to buy boules. Later, bakers began creating the baguette and the ficelle, a skinny baguette extracted from the French word for "string."*

FACING THE TABLE OF CONTENTS: *For all the apparent affluence at the Palace of Versailles, only Louis XIV had use of a bathroom with running water. And powder rooms were intended strictly for powdering one's wig. The antique marble basin is from Pittet Architecturals and Antiques. The iron gates are from TMG Artisan. Both companies are Dallas-based.*

Contents

Acknowledgments

When it comes to producing a book, the credits are endless. Many people play a part in the success of a book.

Madge Baird has been my editor *par excellence* for nearly all of my seven design books. My gratefulness continues to grow for her expertise and encouragement, which I treasure along with her friendship. In addition, I hardly take for granted the efforts of Marty Lee, vice-president of production, Kellie Robles, director of special sales, and Dennis Awsumb, national accounts manager.

Nor do I take for granted the effort the following designers and architects put into helping create the smart, eye-catching, and satisfying rooms that make up this book: Roberto G. Agnolini, Bette Benton, David Corley, Richard Drummond Davis, Vicki Crew, Sherry Hayslip, Bree Hyatt, Karin Lanham, Heidi Ledoux, Lucy Ledoux, Holly Lydick, Tammy Michaelis, Roberta Peters, Marilyn Phillips, Alix Rico, Andrea Smith, Cole Smith, Aline Steinbach, Julie Stryker, Chris Van Wyk, Deborah Walker, and Thomas Weber.

Tight of clock in the family room from Paris Antiques, Santa Fe, New Mexico.

OPPOSITE: *A resplendent* bibliothèque—*crafted in Italy true to the rare nineteenth-century original—filled with a sprawling collection of cream ware from England is worthy of pride of place. The antique Kerman rug has a tribal pattern indigenous to the western section of Iran.*

I appreciate, too, the help of those whose educated eyes assisted on photo shoots, especially Tara Kohlbacher, Zaneta Moreno, Dianne Querbes, Paul Rico, Carrie Taylor, and Liz Lank Williamson. And, thank you, Scott Jacques, Kelly Phillips, and Alix Rico for suggesting residences to shoot.

One of the nicest aspects of writing a book is the opportunity to meet and get to know so many interesting people on both sides of the Atlantic Ocean. Special thanks, therefore, goes to those here and abroad who opened the doors to their impressive *maisons* and permitted me to share the architectural splendor that served as a backdrop for their style and creativity: Roberto Agnolini, Bette Benton, Tracy and Richard Cheatham, Debbie and Eric Green, Mary Alice and Scott Heape, Tavia and Clark Hunt, Heidi and Robert Lydick, Roberta Peters, Alix and Paul Rico, Aline and Erwin Steinbach, to name only a few.

Three books were of great help in deepening my understanding of two influential ladies: *Madame de Pompadour: Mistress of France,* by Christine Pevitt Algrant; *Marie Antoinette,* by Antonia Fraser; and *Louis and Antoinette,* by Vincent Cronin.

Also, I am indebted to my two valued assistants, whose myriad skills I cherish: Tara Kohlbacher and Janice Stuenzl.

Finally, I extend a warm thank-you to you, the reader. Your flair for fusing the accoutrements of assorted cultures was the inspiration for this book.

Introduction

Conventional wisdom has it that we cannot have the best of all worlds. But this is just not so. As if to prove the point, no dwelling with impeccable "bone structure," flat-screen televisions, wine cellar, and beds dressed in fine linens is complete these days without an enviable mix of treasures, however modest, culled from assorted nations circling the globe. A look around, quite simply, opened our minds to the bazaar of choices, giving us cause to disregard this widely held belief. How else to explain the revolution in our leanings, rendering loyalty solely to France passé?

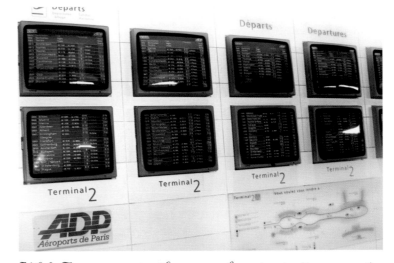

While France remains the source of our inspiration, a monitor at Paris's Charles de Gaulle Airport hints of pleasurable points worth pursuing.

The United States, of course, has long been home to a cadre of furniture designs, encouraging the embrace of whatever manner of stylish living we please. As it is, there are few taboos when either building or expanding our own empires. There are, however, ample challenges. For most, an artful mix of comfort and chic is a priority emblematic of the twenty-first century.

For a generation, at least, the assumption was that sticking to one style of furniture reminiscent of one time period was a safe bet. Whether expressing passion for Louis XV furnishings or admiration for Louis XVI and much-maligned Queen Marie-Antoinette's straight-line splendor, decorating was about one homogeneous look. And now? Moving beyond that notion, we opt to give rooms more character. Having opened the window to a wider world where the possibilities are endless, we layer eras in a single room plus push the borders of design—sculpting distinctive, pleasing interiors that are at once a bit English, a dash Swedish, a trace Italian, to say nothing about ties to other central European countries or even the Far East. Yet most living spaces are so noticeably French that no one would suspect there is tension between the United States and France over Iraq and other issues, much less a weak dollar.

Even if America has not exactly seen eye to eye with *la belle France* recently, a chance survey of sprawling high-rises as well as commanding mansions suggests otherwise. At the center of savvy stateside tastes are sumptuous pieces whose seductive beauty—provenance, painstaking carving, and mellow patina of age—offer a glimpse into our souls aside from more than a modicum of pleasure.

That travel has lost some of its gleam lately is beside the point. Carrying baggage from our past, we make the French connection—fluently mixing and mingling in a way that is far from stylistically limiting—sometimes satisfying our cravings close to home, other times taking far-flung journeys that revolutionize our thinking. Without reservation, we draw from a mélange of cultures, juxtaposing the best the world has to offer with the finest of the French.

OPPOSITE: *Eighteenth-century tapestries worthy of pride of place add to the old-world panache of a stateside salon. The sofa boasts a Coraggio silk, and small pillows flaunt embroidery. The workshops of world-renowned Fortuny (on the largest pillows) are in Venice, Italy.*

Betty Lou Phillips, ASID
Author and Interior Stylist

French Class

A tasting room that is the ne plus ultra of avant-garde chic takes entertaining upscale. The seventeenth-century Italian refectory table is from Orion Antiques, Dallas. Chairs covered in heavily embossed leather are nineteenth-century Portuguese.

French Class

In a world where glitz and grandeur often pose as glamour, the French typically take a more understated approach. Never mind that Louis XIV (1643–1715), the Sun King, shied away from minimalist thinking. Or that he adopted a bigger-is-better, more-is-more mind-set, morphing the modest hunting lodge built by his father Louis XIII (1610–43) into the ostentatious Château de Versailles. The French Revolution quashed desire for jaw-dropping opulence and led to classic simplicity promoted by the new Republic for the benefit of all.

By all appearances well-publicized signs of American affluence—such as bold baubles and imposing domains whose garages host high-performance cars that call further attention to one's success—do not appeal to the steely sensibilities of archetypal French aristocrats. (Although the Revolution supposedly swept away the ruling class, it seems to have not disappeared. The 2005 edition of the French social registry, *Le Bottin Mondain,* which first appeared in 1903, lists 44,000 families, reported *The New York Times*.) In fact, *all* strata of a society that has reveled in egalitarian values for centuries tend to frown on frivolous trappings of wealth that boldly raise one's public profile.

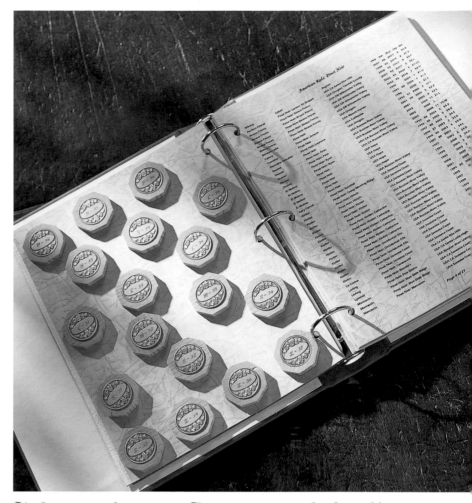

With centuries of experience, France continues to be the world leader in fine wines, but it's clear that American wines are also achieving deserved respect. The octagon-shaped wood pieces and engraved-brass inserts await installation in the cellar.

OPPOSITE: *A cellar—with twelve-foot ceilings and modulated humidity and temperature controls—adjacent to the tasting room accommodates more than three thousand bottles of fine wine within a 130-square-foot area. Ancient fossil ammonites inlaid in the stone floor add to the cave-like ambiance.*

Ever since July 14, 1789, when several thousand angry Parisians demanded justice, storming the Bastille—a medieval fortress widely viewed as a formidable symbol of monarchical power, given that it housed prisoners detained by *lettre de cachet* (royal command) from which there was no appeal—and, in time, overthrowing a monarchy born in 987, the French have had a propensity for linking well-being with equality and leisure, above all else.

For them, a balance between work and play is central to a lifestyle that many believe is superior to what is perceived as the stressful, materialistic, frenzied pace of life in the United States—a notion that probably travels back centuries, say people who think about such things. As it echoes a refrain of Alexis de Tocqueville (1805–59)—the French aristocrat who in 1831, at age twenty-six, spent nine months in the States, and then later rather famously wrote in his *Democracy in America*—that Americans are uneasy with leisure and fixated on accumulating wealth. The way a wide swathe sees it, the old adage "money can't buy happiness" is correct. Instead, it is France's thirty-five-hour workweek, numerous holidays, six-week vacations, and mandatory retirement at age sixty-five, they say, that pave the way to this goal that renders life more fulfilling.

Many proclaim that time spent away from the workplace makes it possible to pursue those priorities that matter most: intellectual, cultural, and, not least, the meaningful relationships all humans crave. It is logical, they maintain, that less work and more play leads to added time with friends, families, and pets, which the vast majority openly admit to thinking of as children—shepherding them to play dates, grooming salons, portraitists, and yes, pricey restaurants where the most mannerly dine at tables set with Limoges porcelain.

In collaboration with nature, dry-stacked Millsap boulders—a soft rubble stone quarried in Millsap, Texas, and available through Roof Tile & Slate Company outside Dallas—lines the walls of a tasting room with double-groin vaulted ceiling abutted by a barrel ceiling over the stairs. In an arched niche sits a stone sink with Herbeau France fittings from Ann Sacks Tile and Stone.

But surprising critics of France's casual work ethics (which often include two-hour lunches), not to speak of its soft economy and high tax rates in return for social services, however generous, is that the French own more second homes than any other people do—as the country's news media likes to remind us.

Americans agree, naturally, that getaways have their merits. But further reflecting the chasm between American and French attitudes, we tend to view vacation homes as overt symbols of wealth—expensive indulgences, pricey or not, often earned through never-ending work weeks and marathon struggles between career and family—while the French see *residences secondaires* as investments in their well-being, giving day-to-day life enhanced meaning. Of course, with nearly twenty percent of the country's sixty-two million inhabitants crowded in the ever-more-congested Ile-de-France—the historic heart of France, including Paris and surrounding seven *départements*—and barely one-fourth living in houses, it's hardly shocking that many people seek a retreat in a *village perdu*, which translates loosely as a rural town in the middle of nowhere or simply away from the proximity of neighbors, as pleasant as they might be.

For years, people fearful of appearing elitist tended to shy away from second-home ownership, given all the talk of restraint, not to mention virulent dislike for suburban sprawl and drawing attention to dissimilar economic means. Helping fuel today's trend is growing acceptance, it seems, that holding court in a spot inherited from a maiden aunt, or even in a place that comes at a price, indicates passion for one's homeland and nothing more.

That said, in France, vacation homes seldom look like vacation homes stateside with cast-off furnishings, old mattresses, outlet linens, and little art. That they are stylish extensions of primary homes is never in question.

With Americans' penchant for remodeling, the number of tasting rooms and wine cellars in this country are growing rapidly. Promoting the movement is an overall rise in American wine drinking following reports that red wine helps prevent heart attacks. Adding to the drama of the wine cellar here is a door designed by Cole Smith, Dallas, who also created the impressive hand-forged iron chandelier, handrail, and espagnolettes *(female busts) embellishing the French doors seen on page 12.*

Vintage barometers—acquired one by one at stateside estate sales—dress up a back stairway, often a forgotten space. No matter that they can't read the weather in heated or air-conditioned rooms.

OPPOSITE: *Warm finishes and collectibles are the foundation of a kitchen with vintage charm. A pot filler swivels over the range, saving the cook a trip from the sink.*

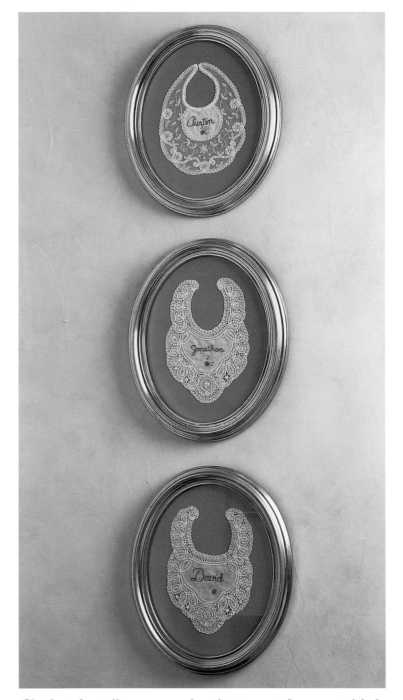

Rather than idle away enveloped in tissue, these special baby bibs hang on the wall of a master bedroom, bringing back memories and sharing links to the family's future.

OPPOSITE: *In seventeenth-century France, the bedroom was where high-level meetings took place. Decades later, Madame de Pompadour removed her* chambre *from the list of public rooms; then it became the private haven that we know. To this day the French keep bedroom doors tightly closed. For guests walking down a hallway to peer into the bedroom of another would be impolite.*

Certainly looks vary widely from one *bonne adresse* to another, taking shape according to one's resources and definition of style. (It could be argued, in fact, that some fall short of American glossy ideals as well as those of *Maison Française*, the leading French shelter magazine.) Rarely, however, do the French stray from their unified approach to decorating, which is faithful to a heritage that has long spurned royal excess.

Exactly as Louis XIV intended, quality still reigns. Whether a storied *mas* (farmhouse) outside Provence's ancient walled city of Avignon, a *folie* (gentleman's getaway perfect for romantic rendezvous) along a stretch of Normandy's legendary coastline, or an *appartement* tucked in a nineteenth-century *hôtel particulier* in the busy capital—now mostly divided into privately owned *primary* residences—chic, comfortable, welcoming spaces, some less formal than others, do the late monarch proud.

Some people, surely, find it hard to resist bargains in the fabled *Marché aux Puces de Saint-Ouen*, the vast flea market on the northern outskirts of Paris that lures tourists *en masse,* or in *L'Isle-sur-la-Sorgue*, the

Taking advantage of a master bedroom's spaciousness, a bibliothèque, *dating back to the nineteenth century offers an unexpected place for storing fine linens. The shelves are fabric-lined to avoid chances of snagging.*

OPPOSITE: *In a room fit for royalty, a* baldaquin *presides over the bed. Cantilevered from the ceiling, it adds architectural definition, while an array of fabrics indulges a passion for blue.*

antique-hunting paradise in the Lubéron region of Provence, where more than 250 *brocanteurs* (dealers in used goods) crowd between branches of the Sorgue River.

Many more, though, shun temptation and instead buy the finest household linens and furniture they can manage—allied by schooling started well before adolescence, when most learned to identify and value beautiful things. When the price of what is desirable is out of reach, they would rather do without than compromise their ideals and then be fraught with regret. For in their view, instant gratification begets short-lived joy—almost without fail, equating to a pricey lesson with obvious drawbacks.

Back in the eighteenth century, France astonished the world with her exquisite craftsmanship, setting standards of excellence unseen before in Italy and Spain, while bringing the style and *bon goût* of her people global acclaim. And it is fair to say that nothing has changed. To this day, the eighteenth century is thought to be the most elegant era in European history, with French furniture from this period justly singled out for praise. Not only that, but the French are hailed as icons of stylistic authority, as they have been ever since helping us win our independence from Great Britain while simultaneously challenging Italy's stylistic might.

With savoir-faire of their own yet barely distinguishable from their parents', each new generation that comes of age ardently embraces the same distinctive artistry that brought the country international fame, drawing from it to judge fine French furnishings and most everything else.

OPPOSITE: *A table draped in a Brunschwig & Fils plaid and a warm mix of furniture create a European ambiance. The panetière—a small hanging cupboard—once stored bread.*

ABOVE: *Houseguests have a retreat all their own—filled with the charm of the French countryside. The same Brunschwig & Fils toile de Jouy blankets both the walls and bed.*

BELOW: *Detail of the bed skirt. Carpet is from Karastan.*

OPPOSITE: *Chairs in the style of Louis XV add to the tranquil ambiance of a guest room. The operable window treatment guarantees privacy and offers the option of sleeping late.*

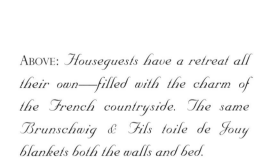

The living room sofa, in a striped cut velvet by Nobilis, is a Cameron Collection design. Churchill chairs are from Rose Tarlow, Los Angeles. Nineteenth-century Italian urns from Brian Stringer Antiques, Houston, adorn the mantel. The coffee table from Biff Agee, Houston, began life as an eighteenth-century Italian gilt-wood bench; the mirrored top is also old. Designer Marilyn Phillips happened upon the nineteenth-century Oushak—from Turkey—at Carol Piper Rugs, Houston.

It is, in fact, both recognized and accepted in antiques shops around the posh Quai Voltaire, on the Left Bank of the Seine across from the Louvre, and in shops more modest throughout the provinces that the French can be demanding critics. Armed with the ability to distinguish between fine and mediocre, it is as if with every choice made, most are intent not only upon imbuing the next generation with a deep appreciation of beauty but also upon assuming responsibility for the ongoing glory of France.

Whether yearning for a major piece of furniture, work of art, or treasured object, reverence for the past exerts a pull so strong that it is unthinkable, for many, to live among meaningless pieces with no ties to their heritage or, worse, in a house pulled together at a hurried pace with furnishings that fail to tell a story or lack familiar signs of wear.

While offerings to which we are heirs that are not exactly what we fancy tend to linger only until we can afford to subtly bid them *au revoir* at the door, in French minds, heirlooms handed down from caring ancestors deserve better, far better. And why not? For who's to say, that any armoire—emblematic of French country life—irrelevant of condition, isn't worthy of preferential treatment given the memories it invariably stores? Or that an inherited commode doesn't somehow appear more cherished when prominently placed on herringbone parquet, whether time has taken a toll or not?

Espousing family history also gives the impression that a setting has evolved piece-by-piece over time—long a decorating dictum. Predictably, then, rooms are works in varying stages of progress, hinting at possibilities. But while some people bide their time, coyly waiting for wishes to be fulfilled, others deliberately choose > 45

A pair of nineteenth-century carved-walnut fauteuils *(upholstered armchairs with open sides) from the Paris Flea Market flaunts a chenille by Beaumont & Fletcher. The* tric trac *gaming table originated during the reign of Louis XV. A Florio Collection embroidered silk taffeta from India heightens the living room's drama. Reportedly, that country's textile cottage industry employs 85 million people.*

Bookcases encircle a dining room table from France, an eighteenth-century chandelier from Italy, and chairs covered in a Lee Jofa damask, produced in the United States. Anchoring the room is a late-nineteenth-century prayer rug, not only unique in size but also with each side having its own distinct pattern rather than being a mirror image. It is from Carol Piper Rugs, Houston. The stained-glass window is original to the early-twentieth-century house.

ABOVE: *A château tile is sited over the range.*

CENTER: *Tiles in the Butler's pantry.*

BELOW: *A once-narrow stairwell borrows space from the kitchen and creates a dramatic entrance to the wine cellar.*

OPPOSITE: *A newly renovated kitchen with the conveniences of today but the charm of an earlier time rivals any France might offer. At Versailles, food traveled nearly a kilometer from the kitchen to the king's table. Here, an extra prep sink services a freestanding island.*

Although wine bars are one of today's hottest trends, some homeowners prefer hosting more intimate gatherings among antiques that lend an old-world air. Eighteenth-century table is Italian. Chairs from Country French Interiors, Dallas, wear original leather and Roger Arlington fabric.

OPPOSITE: *An unassuming banquette flanked by timeworn antiques suits tony surroundings and offers the perfect spot for reading the morning paper. Nineteenth-century crystal chandelier is French; it is from The Gray Door Antiques, Houston.*

Destined to become family heirlooms are a Patina bed and writing table hand-painted in Italy. Beacon Hill fabric bedecks the windows; coverlet fabric is from Great Plains. Dallas-based artisan David Lyles gave the master bedroom walls depth and texture with a translucent glaze.

Like mother, like daughter. Some traits run deep—such as a taste for Etamine, Parisian fabrics, Porthault bed linens, and pretty rooms. The mirrored chest with floral motif is verre églomisé (with glass painted and gilded on the reverse side). It is from the Paris Flea Market. Equally valuable, and perhaps even more meaningful, is the painting by the young girl's maternal grandmother.

to allow one idea to inspire another, letting their visions slowly take shape. And still others simply prefer living in studied simplicity—with mirrors multiplying sparse furnishings set among flowers from a nearby Métro stop—at least for the time being.

Whatever the reason, further underscoring the pressure to think twice before infusing a room with furniture is a deterrent ingrained in the national psyche: more than necessity must prompt the desire to buy.

It is not that need isn't important. However, in a nation where perception is an issue taken seriously, not only is it the prevailing view that an empty space lets others know one hasn't yet happened upon anything fine enough to warrant a purchase, but sparse furnishings point out that setting has not been amassed overnight.

It is irrelevant, apparently, that a faithful reproduction with detailing true to the period of the original costs less than an antique one hundred or more years old. Experts are not shy about letting the world know that, in their view, it is *impossible* to replicate early cabinetmaking with elegant joinery when no screws or nails were used, much less the patina of age—a distinctive luster resulting from centuries of exposure to heat, humidity, light, and oil from hands. This helps explain why furniture with ties to the *ancien régime* has long been held in such high esteem and is the province of savvy investors. But it surely does little to help today's dealers and artisans who wrestle with the challenge of selling the new, that is, pieces crafted later than the nineteenth century or even a few decades ago.

No matter that some new pieces may very well be finer than those antique, since age alone is by no means a guarantee of workmanship, construction, finish, or value. Indeed, just because a piece is handcrafted rather than machine made does not assure quality. Worth depends on several discernable features, in addition to the type of wood used, the condition, and much like today, demand.

A door in Goult, a sun-dapped Provençal village legendary for its charm and beauty.

Holding most everything a Provençal dining area needs is a buffet dating back to the eighteenth century. Above it, from the same era, hangs a full-size rendering called a "cartoon" that once served as a model for a tapestry. Until the mid-nineteenth century, the dining room was not commonplace in American homes.

OPPOSITE: *A villa in the heart of Provence boasts a limestone mantel hand carved by local artisans.*

As it happens, purists could care less that large châteaux throughout the country have gradually given way to more manageable *maisons* and *appartements* with smaller rooms. Or that a richly carved wood piece looks as if it might more readily adorn a castle than a flat with a view of the Eiffel Tower. Indifferent to changing times, scale is paramount. Practiced eyes send the message that furniture with presence is as *recherché* now as when Louis XVI and Marie-Antoinette reveled in the sumptuous splendor of Versailles. Though interiors have a much more approachable ambiance than the era associated with the pair would suggest, noble proportions add to the allure.

Clearly, tastemakers don't waste time fretting over whether or not furnishings match. In their world, harmony is more important than conformity, and the unexpected makes the most confident, stylish statement.

But, of course, it is perfectly acceptable for those who choose to start with, say, a late aunt's identical candelabra whether it is a dinner for family or friends—especially when that late aunt lived on the avenue Foch and helped shape one's design sensibility.

However, an array of great-grandmother's sterling silver Christofle flatware or Cristal Saint Louis puts an even more glamorous spin on *any* occasion, not only the milestones of life. Forsaking five-piece place settings of the same china adds to the aura of sophistication. Likewise, drawing chair frames from different eras and styles earn points for personal panache.

Those who reject the matchy-matchy take pride in touting disparate elements that surprise and charm. They don't feel compelled, for example, to unearth similar side tables to flank a settee, any more than like lamps. This is not to suggest that lamps do not finish at the same height. A sweeping glance confirms that most typically do.

Street markets in the South of France personify the spirit of the region with fresh fruits, vegetables, cheeses, olives, and more.

Texture has a reputation for shaping rooms, much as color—whose opposites attract. A bedroom in Provence is awash in signature extremes—hard and soft, refined and relaxed, light and heavy—creating harmony, which is the ultimate goal.

On the opposite side of the room, a nineteenth-century nursing chair stands near the tub. In addition to thick, fresh scented towels, the French gravitate to those called nib d'abeille (nest bee) for their exfoliating properties. In the States, the same towels are referred to as "honeycomb."

OPPOSITE: *In a bath where the palette doesn't stray from the neutrals, frills are kept to a minimum.*

Let it suffice to say that in France collecting is a national pastime—some would call it a personal mania. Taking to the streets in search of antiques is rooted in desire to preserve the French Republic's artistic treasures, both for oneself and for one's children. But the thrill of the chase is also addictive.

Even the most zealous contend, however, that less is more. There is indeed a fear of cultural backlash against ostentation, but Napoléon's (1769–1821) opinions also remain influential. Persuasively, he long ago advised his followers, "Everything that is big is beautiful." And it remains the French mantra. From early on, Gauls are schooled in an ethos that asserts: one extravagantly scaled *objet d'art* draws the eye and is more readily appreciated than a crowd of small indulgences that beg to be viewed up close.

While arranging decorative objects in an artful, seemingly effortless way, it is as if many set out to prove that less can definitely be more. Tightly edited groupings make a strong statement when congregated together rather than scattered around the room. To be sure, the French do not leave placement to chance. Truth is, everything they do is the result of careful planning. Their exacting nature is a conviction on which both their signature style and the national culture rest.

A second home for Americans is set in the Luberon village of Roussilon. It boasts crepi walls—an age-old method that mixes color, plaster, and sand. As a result, there is no need for paint.

Just $1 an issue

▼ DETACH HERE ▼

HOUSE &GARDEN

IS HAVING A VERY SPECIAL WHITE SALE

12 issues $12
Plus $3 postage & handling

❦ *Reply by January 31st to get the Kitchen Issue* ❦

NAME
_____
(please print)

ADDRESS
_____

CITY _____ STATE _____ ZIP _____ APT. _____

☐ I prefer 2 years for $24 (plus $6 postage and handling)
☐ Payment enclosed ☐ Bill me later

J6ASX1

Just $1 an issue

Visit our website at
www.houseandgarden.com

BUSINESS REPLY MAIL

FIRST-CLASS MAIL   PERMIT NO. 107   BOONE IA

POSTAGE WILL BE PAID BY ADDRESSEE

HOUSE
&GARDEN

PO BOX 37635
BOONE IA 50037-2635

Madame de Pompadour

(1721–64)

Jeanne-Antoinette Poisson was born in Paris on December 29, 1721, the first child of Louise-Madeleine de La Motte, wife of François Poisson. There were many, however, who suspected that her birth father was Charles-François Paul Le Normant de Tournehem, a wealthy financier. He set tongues wagging by openly assuming responsibility for her education, which, in addition to studies at an expensive private school, included voice lessons from Jeloitte, the star of the Paris Opéra at the time, and diction instruction from Pierre Jélyotte Crébillon, a famous playwright.

No doubt some of the talk might well have subsided had not Le Normant de Tournehem declared that he was grooming her to become *un morceau de roi,* literally, "a crumb or morsel of the king," though almost certainly he meant a valuable ally in society and at court.

Did she beg to differ? Or revolt? *Au contraire.* As it turned out, she fulfilled his wistful aspirations when no *bourgeoisie* had been elevated to such a public post as the official mistress of the king.

So how did she rise to *maîtresse en titre*—and in turn become a noteworthy patron of the arts? Unable to obtain an introduction at court, she sought—as if by accident—to catch the eye of Louis XV (1715–74) when he was hunting game in the forest of Sénart, near her château in the Seine Valley, about twenty miles northeast of Paris. Despite her best efforts, however, she failed.

Instead, it was the marriage arranged by her father and Le Normant de Tournehem to the latter's nephew—financier Charles-Guillaume Le Normant d'Étiolles—in 1741 that offered the required respectability, and thus entrée into the glittering social world she craved.

Among thousands of flickering candles at the Yew Ball, a lavish *soirée* at Versailles celebrating the marriage of the dauphin of France, son of King Louis XV and Queen Marie Leszczynska, (historical spellings vary), Madame d'Étiolles danced in the ornate splendor of the *Galerie des Glaces* (Hall of Mirrors) and before the festivities were over waltzed away with the heart of the king.

She credited her achievement to being smart, fashionable, pleasure loving, and, not least, attractive. Though she was much plainer than the beauty portrayed by latter-day artists, how she came to subjugate the king is not in dispute. Profiles of Madame d'Étiolles rarely fail to mention that her

Madame de Pompadour, the influential mistress of Louis XV, graces a pillow hand-painted by Carlsbad, California, artist Jennifer Chapman.

husband was conveniently away on a business trip, giving her ample opportunity to pursue a long-standing goal.

At twenty-three, she and Alexandrine, her nine-month-old daughter, moved into an *appartement* overlooking the perfectly tended *parterres* (formal patterned gardens) suiting the grand exterior of Versailles. Set just one floor above the king's quarters, hers were accessible by a secret staircase tailored to his sexual pleasures. She might have slipped with relative ease into her royal role, as she was a highly educated, sophisticated woman. However, schooling in the strict rules of court etiquette, as well as training in how to walk, talk, and dress, further polished her image—with the intent of quieting Louis XV's advisers, who felt that she failed to reflect his power and even suggested that she might otherwise embarrass him.

As a gift once legally rid of her husband, the king gave her the Château de Pompadour in the quiet hamlet of Arnac, south of the French capital in the Limousin region—an area now celebrated for its Aubusson tapestries and Limoges porcelain. Hence her title, Marquise de Pompadour. And her gift to

A grand salon appears elegant, not stuffy, when glazed oak-paneled walls and a late-nineteenth-century Aubusson carpet lay the foundation for the palette and the furnishings. A carved beech wood settee upholstered in Old World Weavers fabric is from the same era as the carpet.

him? Much like his earlier mistresses, she offered a pleasurable distraction from the boredom and pomposity of court, knowingly or not.

With her considerable ambition neatly hidden behind her ample charm, Madame de Pompadour was not only a worthy rival for a queen faced with the indignity of being forced to share the king but also an adversary of the king's aides and advisers. Notably, she became involved in state policy, urging the appointment of the duc de Choiseul and other ministers who shared her point of view. She also encouraged an alliance with Austria, a move that plunged France into the Seven Years War in 1756, affected most of Europe, and resulted in the loss of Canada to England.

Despite political missteps that had a profound influence on the nation, Madame de Pompadour was a discerning patron of the arts. This would be her lasting legacy. She was a devotee of the theater, interested in the running of Gobelins, the tapestry workshop, and a passionate admirer of Sèvres porcelain. After encouraging the king to move production from the Château de Vincennes in 1759, her influence only grew as she arranged for the building of the esteemed factory in the city from which it would take its name and set about employing top designers and craftsmen.

Beyond that, she deftly spread the Sèvres name across Europe by generously giving the finely glazed porcelain to diplomats from various countries while procuring hundreds of distinctive pieces for herself. (In May 2005, Christie's New York Auction House sold a soft-paste porcelain table fountain that belonged to Madame de Pompadour for $1.8 million.)

At the same time, she became an ardent art collector, lining rooms with the works of the many artists commissioned to paint and sculpt her. (This collection, too, was sold in pieces, not kept intact, when she died.) As a painter favored by Madame de Pompadour, François Boucher (1703–70) gained added acclaim, and that, in turn, helped others recognize him as one of the most illustrious French artists of the eighteenth century. In 1765, he became *premier peintre du roi* (first painter to the king).

The rococo style that would later be associated with the reign of Louis XV first appeared about 1730. But as the persuasive force behind pushing the king to move his court from Versailles to Paris and permitting nobles to live in their own houses, Madame de Pompadour also deserves credit for the period's hallmark interiors. For in keeping with royal whims, the court moved the king's prized possessions from one domicile to the next. And to

One of the pair of consoles in the style of Louis XVI—in the salon *on the preceding overleaf. Fabric from Scalamandré covers the bench.*

her it was clear that this latest destination demanded refined, shapelier silhouettes befitting living areas more modestly scaled than the vast, lofty spaces of glittering Versailles.

Patronizing the top *marchands-merciers* (dealers in works of art and antiques) on the ultrachic rue du Faubourg Saint-Honoré, she sought to replace heroic-proportioned, baroque ceremonial furnishings with graceful chairs, approachable *canapés* (settees), and regally carved commodes. For her, however, gracious living was about more than a savvy mix of fabrics, pastel paint, and carefully chosen furniture. Whereas Louis XIV chairs stiffly lined the walls, she urged that seating float—to further the art of conversation. Because she was mistress of the house, her authority went unchallenged.

No matter that her head-spinning ascension from modest beginnings to irresistible mistress had stunned the royal court—her influence spread. As a result, artisans from across Europe settled in Paris in hope of providing smaller, exquisitely crafted, elegant

ABOVE: *Tight of ceiling treatment.*

BELOW: *For Madame only; a powder room (unseen) is for Monsieur.*

OPPOSITE: *Nestled off the entry is a powder room that rivals the Ritz Hôtel in Paris.*

furnishings to the court of Louis XV, the king's subjects, and Madame de Pompadour, naturally. Many pieces commissioned by Louis XV still tended to be quite lavish—inlaid with exotic-wood marquetry and decorated with gilt-bronze mounts. But few would argue that Madame de Pompadour's unerring taste clearly set a new tone for more stylish decorating.

Rock crystal chandeliers sparkled in rooms awash in pastel velvets from Amiens, silks from Lyons—the heart of the country's production—and *faïence* (fine, glazed ceramics) from Rouen and Sceaux. Wood marquetry flooring replaced floors fabricated from stone, while marble walls gave way to carved paneling, painted or varnished, prompting a style known as *rocaille* to spread rapidly throughout Europe.

Putting her innate flair to good use, Madame de Pompadour focused on fashioning a perfect world for the king. When not organizing a swirl of entertaining performances followed by after-theater suppers, she shared his interest in architecture. Together they founded and built the École Militaire (Royal Military Academy), where young men without means could be trained to become accomplished officers, and created, too, the Place Louis XV, one of the French capital's most beautiful squares, now the Place de la Concorde.

Additionally, the pair worked with architect Ange-Jacques Gabriel (1698–1782) on designs for the Petit Trianon at Versailles, remodeled the Petits Cabinets and rooms soon branded the Petits Appartements, plus added a wing to the palace of Fontainbleau, south of Paris.

With ample competition for her role as *maîtresse en titre*, by 1751 Madame de Pompadour no longer aroused Louis XV's ardor. Yet not one to be cast off easily, she continued to influence the king long after their passionate seven-year affair ended. In honor of their unwavering friendship, he afforded her the power and respect surely due the world's undisputed arbiter of taste and style. After moving her into an apartment on the first floor of the palace, he bestowed upon her the title of duchess in 1756. Later, he named her a lady-in-waiting to the queen.

As she lay dying, at only forty-two, the king remained at her bedside. Then, because court etiquette forbade him from attending her funeral, he stood in the pouring rain tearfully watching her cortège from a balcony overlooking the Place d'Armes. "That was the only tribute I am able to pay her," he reportedly said to his valet.

Making a positive first impression are the doors to a private residence on the Avenue Montaigne, in Paris's ritzy eighth arrondissement.

Pursuing Glamour and Ease

A burnished terra-cotta palette, hand-painted beams, and custom bed turn a spacious master suite into an intimate space. Embroidery adds a refined finishing touch to the mix of Nancy Corzine and Great Plains fabrics.

Pursuing Glamour and Ease

Point Zéro des Routes de France *set in the shadow of the regal Cathédrale Nôtre-Dame.*

Paris may not be the geographical center of what the French proudly call their *hexagone,* but it is indeed the hub of much of France's cultural, educational, financial, and political power. Shedding light on how the people have long viewed their capital is an easy-to-miss octagonal plaque centered in the shadow of the towering Cathédrale Nôtre-Dame on the Île de la Cité, encircled by the Seine. Set in well-worn remnants of medieval roads, it marks *Point Zéro des Routes de France.* From here, the country unfurls; cobbled streets wind from the regal twelfth-century church to the far reaches of the French Republic. Distance is calculated authoritatively away from this spot and back to it, giving the City of Light undeniable stature.

It seems entirely apt, then, that Parisian flair echoes across the country, driving public taste. Nowhere in the republic, after all, is style practiced more passionately—or with as much confidence—than in the capital, the most populous and wealthiest area of France. And even though *"Le plus ça change, le plus c'est la même chose,"* ("The more things change, the more they remain the same") is an adage that most live by, in the last decade or so things have changed in ways *unrelated* to the city's shifting social and ethnic composition. (There are no official statistics on exactly how mosaic the diversity has become, since French law prohibits official censuses from collecting such data as birthplace, race, religion, or ethnicity—in part because of the Nazis' use of government records during World War II to identify those Jewish. But most French feel an influx of immigrants with different tastes and needs are now threatening both the economy and their identity. This is one reason

OPPOSITE: *In a sunroom off the master bedroom on the preceding overleaf, French doors open to the sound of water coming from the fountain.*

ABOVE: *Copper is a staple in French kitchens, mostly because it heats quickly and evenly at low temperatures and then cools quickly.*

BELOW: *Tile on the kitchen countertop is from Tesserae Mosaic Studio, Dallas.*

OPPOSITE: *Anchoring a well-equipped kitchen is a red Lacanche range from the village by the same name in the Côte d'Or region of Burgundy, an area known for its fine food and wine. An ample island meets multiple demands.*

voters rejected the draft European Union constitution on May 29, 2005.) Lately, like-minded generations of style setters have a different, more modern view of luxury that most can't help but notice.

To be sure, opulent, overly grand is a bit too serious for most everyone's likes. And over-decorated is clearly out of favor, suiting neither the times nor the desire for discreet elegance far from the glitz of Versailles. The issues that caused such a stir when

"Chalkboard" paint can add pizzazz to any number of things, including the upper portion of this brick-red door. A touch of wit stocks the walk-in pantry and makes staples highlighted in English, French, and Spanish easy to find.

the Bourbon monarchs ruled were different from public concerns today, but the attitudes of most Parisians are much the same. With ongoing sympathies to the ideals of the French Revolution, those who see themselves as symbols of their class blatantly disregard the notoriously lavish, over-the-top extravagance that preoccupied the image-obsessed *ancien régime*. Although there is still much to boast about as fine furnishings remain a mainstay of French style, ornate has gone the way of the guillotine and good taste is not about personal wealth.

Instead, a deft mix of glamour and ease have become the new symbols of exalted status. And the capital's historic architecture is the link. Soaring ceilings, lofty windows, and plaster walls coupled with deep chiseled moldings and patterned wood floors are the framework of patrician *hôtels particuliers,* the once-grand single-family residences indigenous to Paris that have been converted into individual flats worthy of note.

OPPOSITE: *A multitasking project room with plenty of storage space stands ready to tackle whatever a busy household presents. On the walls: Sherman Williams' "Chalkboard Black." Ceiling fan is from Mathews Fan Company, Libertyville, Illinois.*

Granted, not every *appartement* hidden behind heavy, lacquered doors—in a city where apartment dwelling is the norm—is an architectural gem. Design aficionados consider low ceilings, meager moldings, and floors demanding wall-to-wall carpeting the nemesis of glamour, much like a bevy of critics view heat, humidity, and the sun's rays as the chief adversaries of works of art and books. (It's not surprising, then, that these are the very rentals marketed to Americans and other foreigners.)

The pale, locally quarried Lutecian limestone façades we associate most strongly with *la ville lumière* are Georges-Eugène Haussmann (1809–91) creations designed for the vast middle class who suffered from a severe housing shortage after the Revolution. During the Second Empire (1851–70), Napoléon Bonaparte's nephew, Louis Napoléon Bonaparte III (1808–73), hired Baron Haussmann to metamorphose the shattered, war-torn city from a bleak, crowded metropolis where living conditions were dreadful into the most elegant, imperial city on earth. And, indeed, his city-planner rose to the challenge.

Borrowing ideas from modernized London while taking inspiration from architect Andrea Palladio (1508–80), who stunned Europe with his insistence on proportional relationships and then documented his beliefs in *The Four Books of Architecture,* Haussmann and an army of 14,000 laborers fanned out across Paris. Together they flattened thousands of buildings—some damaged, others neglected, still others health hazards—widened streets, installed news kiosks under freshly planted trees, created transportation systems and public parks with fountains and benches, and triumphantly developed a sophisticated system that dispatched running water into newly constructed towering structures with noble airs.

The distinctive silhouettes of Haussmann's exteriors are easy to identify. Not only are they classically

Some dogs relish an outdoor run; others are thankful for a stylish bed. And though it has been said that nowhere is the impulse to spoil one's loyal friends greater than in France, it is in America where those living in luxury have a room of their very own.

symmetrical, but they are also beautifully proportioned, with elegant masonry and thick stone walls rising no more than six stories tall. Roofs as well as rainspouts are fashioned from zinc rather than lead. Windows are deliberately equal in size. Hand-forged iron railings lend grace to balconies on the second and fifth floors. And only on *close* examination is it apparent that details differ in the stonework and doors, so there is visual harmony on both banks of the Seine.

Amidst such architectural splendor, most Parisians see no need for added grandeur. The ormolu (gilded bronze ornamentation) and gilding (gold decoration) favored by the Sun King and his many mistresses work for only a few. Reflecting the need for simpler lives, without the hoopla, less-formal Louis XV and Louis XVI furnishings, not necessarily from the period, pay homage to design philosophies in the Île-de-France.

In rooms exuding the trademark restraint and polished taste for which the French people are famous, opulent red velvet appears more than a bit excessive. And heavy, layered drapes with cornices, swags, and pelmets? Too showy. Many not only consider these the height of pretension but also see them as preventing natural light from flowing into rooms. There is a widespread feeling, too, that elaborate window treatments have a way of visually lowering ceilings while making windows appear shorter than they are. For similar reasons even valences are becoming passé.

To project old-world élan, chic *salons* parade the requisite accessories: majestic armoires with regally curved bonnets, glittering rock-crystal chandeliers not always as celebrated as Baccarat—their aristocratic cousin—and hand-woven Aubusson and Savonnerie carpets that are lauded, if only because they have survived the French Revolution and ravages of two World Wars.

A powder room in a newly constructed house evokes a traditional feeling with beaded-board tile topped by wall covering from F. Schumacher. Sconces are from Restoration Hardware and the towels are by Waterworks.

In those *salons* that want for nothing, faded tapestries look down from walls. There are billowing taffeta curtains duly adorned with *passementerie* (fringe, braid, or tassel trim) tumbling from iron rods, *fauteuils* (upholstered armchairs with open sides) sometimes wearing original paint—no matter how faint—and fresh-cut blooms straight from the garden. With little fanfare, *boiserie* glazed pale gray, gray-green, or gray-blue offers the perfect backdrop for valued *objets d'art,* ancestral portraits, and cherished books, as well.

As if on a mission to keep the nation's rich cultural heritage from falling prey to a wave of tourists, dealers, collectors, and—not least—American decorators and their clients, tributes to France lend further presence. But even with the propensity of some to attract more than their fair share of attention, most *salons* are neither swank nor stuffy giving the impression of being off-limits or reserved for parties after-five. Quite the opposite. Putting fragile objects on proud display like artifacts in one of the country's thirty-four national museums is viewed with distaste in most circles. Rather, convention dictates that settings must be family-friendly, spots where dogs may doze and children can bring smiles to faces.

It would be easy, of course, for France's artistic riches to overshadow a room's unassuming treasures, but most do not. Some flea-market finds, to be sure, are more interesting than others. But with fastidious attention to detail embedded in the culture, the French manage to elevate the ordinary to varying degrees of prominence, sometimes making the common difficult to ignore. It is a tradition spawned in the seventeenth century, when Louis XIV and his visionary finance minister, Jean-Baptiste Colbert, established a strictly controlled guild system that regulated the work of artisans, holding their specialties to the highest set of principles and reinforcing the need to give thought to every detail, however subtle.

ABOVE: *With the old-fashioned medicine cabinet now passé, a smart solution for stylish bathroom storage is a vintage apothecary cabinet with a steel finish and brass knobs. This one hails from France.*

OPPOSITE: *Just because it is called a pharmacy chest doesn't mean it can't host towels, oils, and creams unlikely to be found in the average drugstore.*

Not only did Dallas-based artist Kay Fox lavish attention on this side of the nursery, but so did the child's mother, who planned both closed storage and open cubbyholes to house everything her young son could need.

OPPOSITE: In a nursery that looks as if it has just stepped out of a children's book, a rug from Pottery Barn Kids sprawls on the floor.

Splish, splash. Look at this tub. Credit goes to Tesserae Mosaic Studio, in addition to the little boy's parents, of course.

OPPOSITE: *A special space created just for guess who? Bubbles add a touch of whimsy. Glass tiles are from Waterworks.*

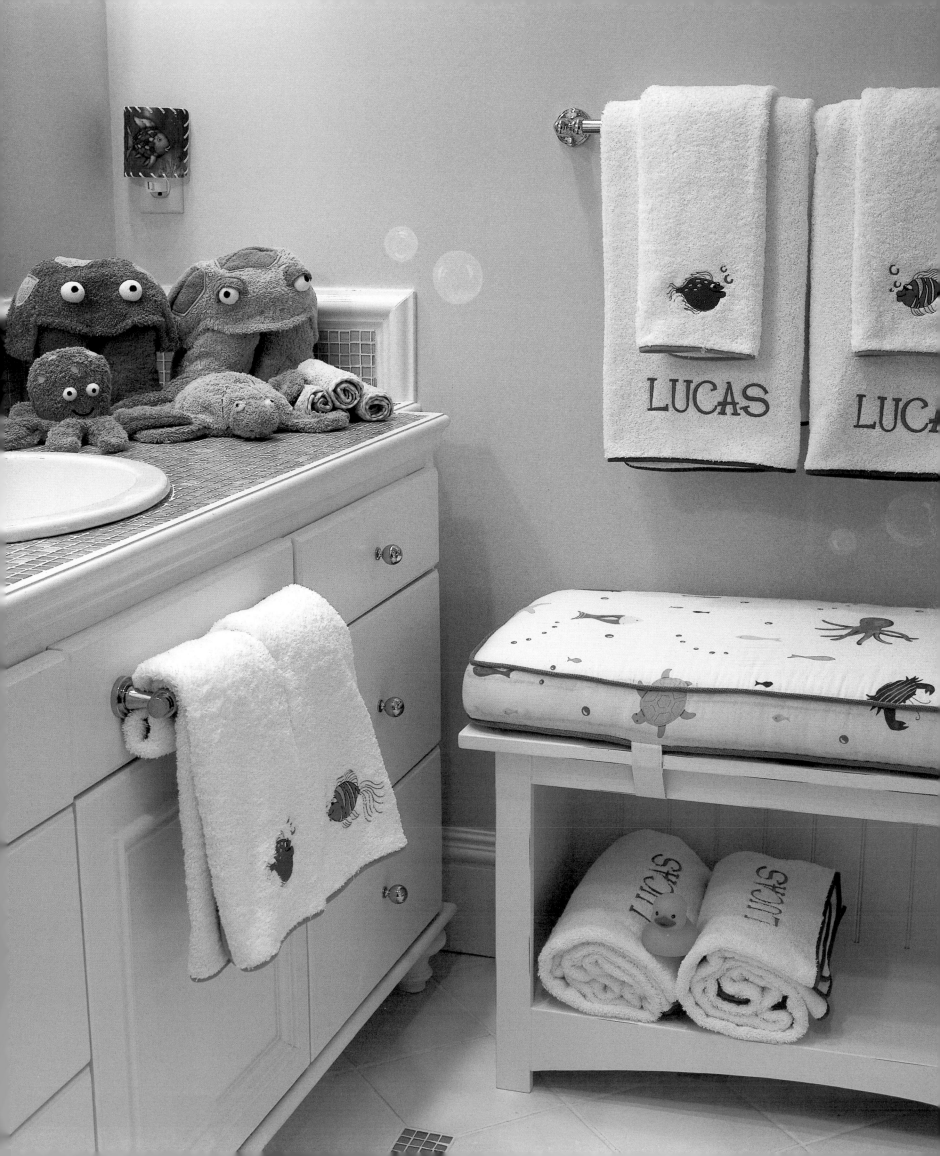

Imbued with respect for the discreet, Gauls have a way of quietly employing flattering tactics to add richness to their rooms. Pairing fragments steeped in the past in a manner fitting the present, vintage textile remnants become plump pillows. Slipcovers flaunt dressmaker details—piping, corner pleats, and tailored skirts—camouflaging weary furniture when not protecting luxurious fabrics hidden underneath. Throws tossed nonchalantly over the backs and arms of sofas and chairs wrap furnishings in warmth. Generously proportioned upholstery with down-and-feather fill encourage friends to linger. Humble antiques morph into splendid lamps. Pale pink silk lines lampshades decked in braid trims, creating a romantic glow.

Where better to come ashore and camp out for the night than in a playroom destined to delight? Denim shade fabric is by Henry Calvin Fabrics. Oars sailed from The Uncommon Market, Dallas, to Straight Stitch, fabricators of the window treatment.

A tight of the window treatment.

OPPOSITE: *Putting a spin on tradition, a Dallas teen opts for high-five style, slam-dunk comfort, and a modern air in his room. Not unlike his friends, he has defined areas for listening to music, studying, and sleeping. Once Garland Kitchen Solutions in Garland, Texas, turned a marble-filled sheet from Architectural Systems, Inc., in Manhattan, into a headboard, he had the makings of a mega cool room.*

A bulletin board records bright moments as well as a few sporting events with unhappy endings.

OPPOSITE: *In an aim to please, a home that pays tribute to international influences sports American spirit. Lockers and side table from Pottery Barn Teen store treasures. Designers Guild fabric stretches across the wall. The ladder leads to a loft.*

Hardly a detail is without significance, for that matter. Mirrors in all shapes and sizes enlarge small spaces, while larger rooms bask in reflected glamour, communicating an elegant, uptown spirit. Fabrics with a glossy finish catch the light. Art hung *salon* style—stacked high on walls—benefits from settings where it can readily be viewed up close.

A smart-looking painted piece air-freighted from Venice lends added distinction while mingling amicably with furnishings that span the centuries: an eighteenth-century commode from the beguiling rococo period (1730–60)—when Louis XV and his renowned mistress, Madame de Pompadour, had great influence on the decorative arts—a chic neoclassical chair, and fabrics from the finest mills.

Mixing periods is common practice, easing formality. But a leopard print may also sweep away the seriousness of a space by making the glamorous appear more relaxed. Elsewhere, a mirrored table from the 1940s can lighten the mood. Although the German occupation of France (1940–44) is not forgotten, in the last decade or so, furnishings from the period have shed their stigma as visible reminders of World War II.

In flats as fashionable as the occupants who inhabit them, the culture and style pair well. Clinging to their ways, Parisians lean toward eighteenth-century serene tones—from rich cream, parchment, caramel, pearl gray and taupe, to icy shades of blue, lavender, and pink with just a hint of color. For all its beauty, Paris is often shrouded in soft gray cloud cover, or *la grisaille*, as the French call it. In pallid light, many find riotous patterns and saturated color combinations more than faintly off-putting, especially during the winter months when it gets dark in mid-afternoon. Sizzling, vivid palettes with a spicy mix of patterns, they assert, better suit the strong light in the South of France, where they can bask in the sun.

Bonding the bedroom and bath: A high-style washstand fabricated by Garland Kitchen Supply and sanitas wall covering from RTF International in Fairlawn, Ohio. But the biggest hit is the rows of small red stitches that form stripes, hand painted by Charles Howard to resemble those on a baseball.

ABOVE: *Exercising her creativity, designer Deborah Walker came up with a vanity handcrafted to look like furniture. A Fortuny motif inspired the hand-painted tile commissioned from Marcia Ketchum at Antique Floors, Dallas. The towels are by Matouk. Vendors, these days, are marketing the gram count of towels—the higher the number per square meter, the heavier and more absorbent the towel—much as they have been promoting sheets with high thread counts.*

BELOW: *Guest bath walls go from plain to pretty with decorative molding and stenciling. The antique-style porcelain tub is from The Sunrise Specialty Company, Oakland, California. Not until the mid-eighteenth century did Versailles have rooms that accommodated bathtubs. In fact, Louis XVI was the first French monarch to have the use of a proper bathroom.*

MICHELANGELO DRAWINGS

MICHELANGELO SCULPTURE

MICHELANGELO PAINTINGS

For those who like to read in bed, the plain vanilla lamp shade is out. A shade lined in gingham adds to the setting's charm. The lamps (one unseen) are from Vaughan.

OPPOSITE: Both the Venetian mirror and the mirrored chest are from the Mews—with fifty shops in its Dallas stable. A Peacock Alley matelassé tumbles down windows and sprawls across the bed. Plump hydrangeas, or hortensia, as the French call them, make this guest room even more inviting.

PRECEDING OVERLEAF: The quickest fix for a tired chest is a hand-rubbed paint finish. Revived, this one now stands ready in the sitting room on the front jacket and on the title page to offer guests ample storage.

Ruching adds a feminine touch to a Louis XVI settee in the salon *opposite.*

OPPOSITE: *Painting an artfully fashioned* salon *with importance is a sophisticated mix of Louis furnishings and exquisite European antiques transported from France.*

Point de Beauvais—*the delicate embroidery favored by Madame de Pompadour—adorns lamp shades hand stitched by nuns in France.*

OPPOSITE: *Twins don't come along every day, nor do nurseries this pretty. Canopies over the cribs are twice the fun. Fabric is from Travers.*

Not surprisingly, a bassinette swaddled and smocked in silk from Travers, Inc., can make a baby smile. The vintage silk fabric covering the Louis XV bergère (fully upholstered armchair with enclosed sides and exposed wood frame) was hand embroidered in a nunnery. Curtains made of antique lace add to the nursery's quiet magic.

OPPOSITE: *Like the Hall of Mirrors at Versailles, this powder room had a humble start. But metallic platinum paint from the Crescent Bronze Powder Company now adds panache to plaster walls, while mirrors reflect a seventeenth-century Italianate table and French commode. The rock crystal basin set is from Sherle Wagner; the engravings are antique.*

Napoléon Bonaparte, Emperor of France, was born on the island of Corsica a year after the island came under French rule. In 1796, he married Rose Tascher, after changing her name to Joséphine. Since she could not bear children, she consented to an annulment in 1809 so he could marry eighteen-year-old Marie-Louise of Austria, niece of Marie Antoinette. Many in France consider Napoléon a genius. His Civil Code is the foundation of Europe's modern legal system. Empire style further distinguishes his reign.

OPPOSITE: A tapestry with roots in the nineteenth century reflects grand French style. Sofa is covered in fabric from Christopher Norman; chairs wear Christopher Hyland.

Never mind that various textures absorb and reflect light differently, or that as the sun moves, the ambiance of a room changes, or even that light shifts with the seasons—throughout France, habitués have a way of creating the aura of romance to soften the harsh edges of daily life.

Because track lighting is jarring—at times casting unforgiving shadows on the face and sometimes calling attention to wrinkles—it is scarce. Instead, layers of candles, sconces, and picture lights, in addition to carefully placed table and floor lamps with low wattage bulbs, add cachet. In pursuit of *la douceur de vivre* (the sweetness of living), manipulating light is key.

Oak beams dating back to fifteenth-century France, hand-carved cabinetry, and limestone countertops lend European charisma to a San Francisco manor. The reclaimed terra-cotta pavers are worn by time.

Trompe l'oeil adds to the appeal of the glass-domed ceiling in the breakfast room.

OPPOSITE: *Régence-style side chairs join a Portuguese table from Hamilton, Los Angeles, in a Bay Area breakfast room. Following the French Revolution, the rooster came to symbolize the people of France, and is thus a favored motif.*

A long, narrow hall, spare as the nave of an early cathedral, offers a quiet spot for enjoying a glass of licorice-flavored pastis—a preferred drink in the outdoor cafés of Provence. Skirted table kerchief is by Coraggio.

OPPOSITE: *Furnishings in scale with the room reflect the proportions of a great hall that brims with culture and appeal. The Louis XIII writing desk, circa 1790, is from William Word Antiques, San Francisco. The wrought-iron torchères are Italian.*

ABOVE: *The town of Calais, on the shores of the North Sea, is the lace capital of France, though Chantilly and Valenciennes are also famous centers.*

BELOW: *Lace for the dormer curtains is from Cowtan & Tout.*

OPPOSITE: *An Ironware International lit à la polonaise (Polish bed) exquisitely layered in Clarence House matelassé, Kravet silk plaid, and Old World Weavers lace hints of romance as bed hangings create a room within a room. Area rug is from Stark Carpets.*

Pastels from the palette of California artist Manuel Cruz transform a once dark powder room into one that exudes beauty. The Italian commode is from Decorative Crafts. Both the mirror and sconces are nineteenth-century French.

OPPOSITE: *Looks can be deceiving. Textured walls are trompe l'oeil in a luxurious master bathroom where a chic dressing table holds court. Fabric is Nancy Corzine. Tassels and trims are by Robert Allen.*

Marie Antoinette

(1755–93)

Maria Antonia was born in Vienna on November 2, 1755, the fifteenth of sixteen children of the Empress Maria Theresa of Austria and her emperor husband Francis I. All six girls in her family were christened Maria, after their powerful mother, and like their brothers had privileged childhoods growing up in the relaxed elegance of Shönbrunn Palace and numerous other Hapsburg castles.

In a deliberate political alliance arranged by her mother, the princess obediently married the Dauphin of France—Louis Auguste, the future Louis XVI—by proxy on April 19, 1770. She was only fourteen, unable to speak French, and ill prepared for the scheming, jealousy, and stifling protocol of the French court. Regardless, two days later, Maria Antonio and her lapdog dutifully began the long journey from Vienna to Versailles in a parade of fifty-seven carriages carrying more than one hundred ladies-in-waiting, dressmakers, servants, chaplains, and doctors.

In the French border town of Strasbourg, in the mountainous Alsace region, Gallic attendants replaced her cortege—and directed that her beloved dog be sent back to Vienna as well. Yet out of respect for her husband, she ceremoniously discarded her clothes, down to her stockings and underwear, and donned much fancier French-made garments. Then,

in an even more deliberate gesture directed at warming the hearts of a people exceedingly hostile to Austria for centuries, she cast aside her given name, becoming forever the more French Marie Antoinette.

Sealing her fate and enduring fame, the princess officially exchanged marriage vows with the sixteen-year-old heir to the French throne at Versailles on May 16, 1770, three days after their first meeting. Her duty, as dauphine, was to give birth to an heir; however, it would be seven years before the marriage was consummated, and 1778 before she finally gave birth to the first of four children. (Numerous biographers would later claim that her husband's impotency was responsible for her extravagant spending, which added to France's already serious economic woes.)

Marie Antoinette became Queen of France when Louis Auguste succeeded his grandfather Louis XV in 1774. Upon assuming the throne, the young king prayed, "Protect us, Lord, for we reign too soon." While possessing unwavering love for France, he lacked the confidence and decisiveness necessary to end the peoples' growing unrest, as well as the wisdom needed to reduce the debt he inherited from over-indulgent relatives known for their lavish spending and storied appetite for war who preceded him in power.

Behind the regal image of the martyred Queen Marie Antoinette painted by California artist Jennifer Chapman is a nineteenth-century fabric the author happened upon in the Paris Flea Market.

With apologies to none, the queen—fashionable, frivolous, and fun-loving—set about creating her own utopia, transforming everything around her to match her taste, needs, and whims. Tainting the emotional climate at Versailles, she banished courtiers who had previously snubbed her, dismissed those in positions founded solely on privilege, and created a hefty number of enemies among those provoked by her changes.

With obvious disdain for court etiquette, she also failed to abide by time-honored rules of conduct. It didn't suit her, for example, to awaken to a roomful of courtiers milling about, much less dress before wandering eyes. She found the ceremony associated with retiring, the *coucher,* equally as objectionable as the morning *lever*.

Relations between the queen and the court became even more strained by her choosing to spend most of her time secluded in the Petits Appartements, hidden rooms once used as servants' quarters. Delighting in the privacy she craved, she mastered playing the harp and welcomed only her children and intimate friends, most of whom were disliked by the rest of the court.

Partly because of the strong resentment her Austrian roots stirred, and partly because she tended to hold herself apart, the French soon made a career out of chronicling Marie Antoinette's faults. Even worse, she was the victim of malicious gossip and fabricated verbal assaults. (She did not, to be sure, utter "Let them eat cake," when told the lower classes were starving. This tale first appeared in *Confessions* by Jean Jacques Rousseau, two years before Marie Antoinette arrived in France—and demonstrates that stories of her thoughtless extravagance might be similarly exaggerated.)

Knowing that Marie Antoinette found the rigidity of the palace stifling, out of compassion the king gave her the Petit Trianon in 1783, which Louis XV had built for Madame Pompadour mid-century. It, as well as the more rustic Hameau, became her personal retreats. Inside the latter, she indulged her fondness for printed cottons, especially toile de Jouy. This distressed the silk manufacturers of Lyon, whose sophisticated textiles were garnering admiration in other aristocratic households.

Having grown up in the relaxed atmosphere of Shönbrunn Palace, Marie Antoinette resisted the pretentious opulence the court deemed appropriate for royalty. Rather than the reigning influences, she preferred less-obtrusive suggestions of grandeur that some thought too faint for the taste of the time, and favored a soft palette of pale greens, blues and violets. To bring added comfort and a more intimate air to the ceremonial rooms of Versailles, the queen opted for neoclassical furnishings, which hardly robbed the palace of glamour. Yet not until Empress Eugénie, the elegant wife of Napoleon III, revived the neoclassical style would people credit Marie Antoinette with building the design's cachet.

The neoclassical style that now bears the name *Louis Seize* had appeared more than fifteen years before Louis XVI ascended the throne. Discovery of the ruins of Herculaneum and Pompeii revealed the simplicity of everyday life in the first century A.D., while the ease of Greek and Roman architecture inspired craftsmen to strip away superfluous flourishes. Madame de Pompadour insisted they also incorporate straight lines whenever possible. Consequently, both Marie Antoinette's leanings and the peoples' weariness of baroque excess were consistent with the decorative arts of the period.

The basic shape of desks, commodes, and small tables did not change, but slender tapered legs and right angles increasingly replaced rococo curves. And rather than motifs suggestive of rocks and shells, bouquet-filled baskets, rosettes, and garlands adorned the finest furniture and fabrics. Popular, too,

For more than 700 years, painted Italian pieces have been a source of national pride. Here a secrétaire *from Ambiance Antiques, San Francisco, sits in a place of honor. Expressive Designs in Redwood City, California, fabricated the iridescent curtains from The Silk Trading Co.*

An early-nineteenth-century French commode from Habité, San Francisco, and limestone steps imbue a new home with the aura of a French château.

Mignon, a tiny Papillion with butterfly ears, is the same breed pictured in some portraits of Marie Antoinette.

were wreaths, urns, and sprays of flowers entwined in ribbons. Most of all, the queen admired those motifs reflecting nature.

At Versailles, Marie Antoinette's passion for flowers was apparent. With a distinct fondness for roses, which would become her personal symbol, she appointed master botanist Pierre-Joseph Redouté (1759–1840) as official illustrator of her favorite blooms. (Later, he would become Empress Joséphine's "artist-in-residence" at Malmaison, in Reuill, outside Paris.) Nonetheless, at the time, most people considered flowers too rustic for table centerpieces. Edible sculptures—temples, fountains, hedges, and large baskets with spun flowers of every description—fashioned from sugar paste were the creative option. Afterward, *biscuit*—unglazed white porcelain closely resembling sugar paste—from the Sèvres factory would replace fragile confections on tables across the Continent.

The Reign of Terror ended the lives of Louis XVI and Queen Marie Antoinette, but her intimate, informal interpretation of elegant, refined neoclassical style remains her legacy.

ABOVE: *A mix of statuary and greenery invites admiration.*

BELOW: *An Aubusson carpet fragment has a new home in the States. The best-known eighteenth-century carpet designer was Pierre-Josse Perrot, who was fond of using shells, acanthus leaves, and floral motifs in his designs.*

A tall nineteenth-century clock stands a world away from the French villa where it once proclaimed everlasting love.

Designer Roberta Peters brings the taste of France to a Bay Area kitchen. Beaumanerie limestone sprawls across countertops and sweeps the floor. When preparing meals, the painting over the range is moved, naturally.

Going Global

Color-saturated walls set a dramatic tone in a salon with roots in the seventeenth century. A company in France that specializes in historical hues discovered the deep, matte red in an Egyptian temple. The pair of Louis XV bergères is upholstered in a Pierre Frey fabric. An antique cast-iron fireback stands in the fireplace.

Going Global

Maybe times have changed. But with echoes of the eighteenth century, we still take our design cues from those on a Grand Tour who traveled widely in Europe and occasionally farther, culling disparate influences for their home interiors. The works of art, rugs, and porcelain they shipped or carted home not only served as special reminders of this valued experience but also helped a decorating scheme fall into place.

The once obligatory tour originated in England but quickly found favor on the Continent. This male-only privilege was the province of every socially ambitious young man's continuing education, not limited exclusively to sons of fortunate lineage who had no need to elevate their social status, or even to those with an affluent upbringing. Depending upon a family's resources, some men roamed the Continent for as many as eight years. Those of more modest means journeyed only a few months. Nearly all, however, struggled to define who they were by where they were en route or where they had been, saying nothing of any youthful yearnings for adventure, which might derail a drive for upward mobility, and a more promising future as a member of the aristocracy. With travel being the era's status symbol, most viewed worldliness as guaranteeing access into the social swirl, if not the ruling class, even if unproven. Being educated in the French capital would also add to one's social clout, the thinking went.

A beloved Brunschwig & Fils toile holds sway in a seventeenth-century château set in the Luberon village of Roussillon. A Rubelli taffeta adorns the bed wall; other walls (unseen) wear a wide blue-and-white linen stripe.

By preserving its architectural strength, the kitchen of a seventeenth-century château retains its original spirit, albeit rearranged. Louis XVI chairs envelop a nineteenth-century Italianate table that previously stood in a Milan library. The collection of antique iron jugs, once used for boiling water, is from India. The white ceramics are from Poitiers, France. The floor is a thick Italian tile that resembles stone. Cupboards have a wenge patina that is indigenous to the central African exotic dark wood.

At the time, Paris was fast becoming the epicenter of culture, the world hub of the decorative arts. Although not the city fixed in imaginations today, it was thought of as a finishing school capable of shaping the thinking,

imparting the sheen of privilege, and exerting strong influence on the dress of those looking to better themselves. Fittingly, then, the City of Light often was the prized first stop on travel itineraries, although those who grew up in France generally headed to Italy.

Most left home with cumbersome steamer trunks in tow, valets to handle personal needs, and tutors who signaled their interest in broadening their knowledge rather than their hope of infiltrating society. Throughout their travels, the men studied art, history, language, and the culture, toiled at fencing and equitation, and not only honed keen appreciation of fine food but also gleaned the charm necessary to brighten most any room. This is not to suggest that all shrunk from a rich night life, only that proper manners, influential connections, and well-cut coats put an elite corps on course to serve at the court of Versailles before eventually packing their belongings and setting out for Italy.

While a select few planned lengthy sojourns >135

Roussillon, one of the most beautiful villages in France, owes its celebrity to its cliffs, the source of the world's largest ochre deposit. Mellow old-world shades of ochre range from oxblood with undertones of brown to pale yellow.

OPPOSITE: *Coral silks from Boussac Fidini Borghi swaddle a striking iron-and-brass bed available from Camille en Provence in Goult, France. The antique carpet is from Iran. Paint is Farrow & Ball.*

ABOVE: *Tight view of mosaic table and Willie the cat.*

BELOW: *A Brunschwig & Fils blue-and-white* toile *(meaning "cloth" in French) dresses an antique child's chair. Craftsmen printed early toiles in blue, red, sepia, or purple on a cream-colored cotton ground. Engraved details didn't show up well in yellow until artisans began stronger shades of the hue.*

OPPOSITE: *Whether embracing family or friends, a solarium adapts to the demands of modern life. And by its very nature, a loft offers a lot of light.*

A Scalamandré toile—"Hunting Party"—running through the center of a throw pillow is flanked by a wine velvet from Sanderson.

OPPOSITE: *Warm tones, stacks of books, and family treasures give this library a cozy feeling.*

A mirrored screen adds instant glamour to a dining room that clearly has nothing to hide but much to admire, including the antique English pedestal table. Unprepared to leave behind the hand-painted wallpaper from Gracie, Inc., New York City, the designer-homeowner moved it to her new home.

A tight of a dining room chair with dressmaker details. Fabric and trim are by Pindler & Pindler.

in Venice, others wound their way southeast to Florence or Rome—the cultural and religious capital of seventeenth-century Europe. Having read about the Pantheon, Coliseum, and other notable Eternal City structures of ancient civilization whose influence had grown steadily, most were eager to view firsthand these popular sources of artistic inspiration.

The dazzling discoveries of the ancient Roman towns of Herculaneum (in 1738) and Pompeii (in 1748), buried in an eruption of Mount Vesuvius, near Naples, during the first century A.D., prompted many to linger in Italy in hope of taking part in an archeological dig. As it was, unearthed frescoed rooms and artifacts were pointedly influencing decorative motifs, furniture styles, and both textile and wallcovering designs. On the Continent and in England, pairing interiors painted dark terra-cotta, or Pompeii red, with striped fabrics became a chic thing to do.

For most, interest in making a Grand Tour waned with the fall of the monarchy at the onset of the French Revolution. But the expedition had left its mark by the late eighteenth century. While spreading classical ideas and sophisticated French style across Europe, it had bridged the gap to the United States, which by then had successfully broken away from Great Britain.

In the States, the Grand Tour continues to thrive. Though short on glamour, 24/7 news coverage, the Internet, and other vehicles of mass communication, such as the telephone, have opened our minds. And a fascination for travel means we think nothing of lugging home a bazaar of influences that bring pleasure, stir memories, and reflect our worldly tastes.

A sterling silver cup called une timbale—often engraved—is a traditional baby gift in France, since the French long believed that silver was protective. Those pictured here celebrate the births of three children, now grown, who have children of their own creating happy memories.

OPPOSITE: A nineteenth-century cupboard from Belgium, flanked by monochromatic toile curtains, serves as a backdrop for breakfast room chairs dispatched from England to surround a farm table from France. An irresistible horse that once stood on a stateside carousel adds to the family's fun.

Unpretentious hand-painted furniture from Sweden's Gustavian period (1772–1809) reflects the light as if getting set to face the country's famously long dark winters. During the summer, however, the sun can rise at 2:00 A.M. Most of Sweden sits at the same latitudes as Alaska, Greenland, and Siberia.

OPPOSITE: Airy textiles, a crystal chandelier, and pale palette reveal the admiration King Gustavus III (1746–92) developed for the neoclassical furnishings of Louis XVI following his lengthy tour of France. Soft shades of gray, blue, and sage typify distinctive Swedish style, as does creamy white, which disguises dining chairs crafted in fir, considered an inferior wood.

A tight at the entrance to the palazzo.

An ancient hand-carved limestone fountain is the centerpiece in a courtyard ideal for entertaining.

OPPOSITE: *Embracing his family's Italian roots, Colorado Springs designer Roberto Agnolini goes global—to restore a Caprino, Italy, palazzo in and out of the family for centuries. (Caprino is nineteen kilometers southeast of Verona, the home of famous lovers Romeo and Juliet.)*

From the twelfth to the fourteenth centuries, iron plaques graced the front entrance to the Cathedral of San Zeno in Verona, Italy. To ward off further damage from bronze disease—an outbreak of small patches of corrosion caused when chlorides and oxygen merge in a damp setting—in 1940 they were removed and recast. The first recast set hangs on the stair wall shown here.

A seventeenth-century underground cave that once stored barrels of wine offers the constant temperature and humidity ideal for stocking and aging wine to this day.

OPPOSITE: *A* soggiorno *(the room where people visit, in Italy) is filled with centuries-old furnishings, including some heirlooms from its past. The seventeenth-century tapestry is from Brussels; the chairs and settee are Italian. The Gothic Revival desk, circa 1840, came from England. Nineteenth-century wood-and-gold-leaf medieval monks are fresh from Thailand.*

It is not every day that a homeowner prepares lunch for the photographer, the author, and her assistant. But, then, shooting in Italy is not an everyday occurrence, so it stands to reason that lunch would not be the usual fare. The village's Saturday-morning market inspired the menu. In Italy, as in France, the midday meal is the most important one.

An updated kitchen, new bathrooms, and furnishings from around the world give a palazzo international pizzazz.

Piranesi views of Roman ruins overlook a sitting room off the bedroom above.

ABOVE: *An antique tablecloth stumbled upon in the Portuguese Madeira Islands—in the middle of the Atlantic 600 kilometers from Morocco—now doubles as a guest room bedcover. The art of lace making developed in Europe in the sixteenth century.*

BELOW: *Detail of sitting area.*

Chinoiserie

Porcelain in a seating area of the master bedroom on page 24.

Tales from China brought back to Europe by missionaries, scholars, and travelers abounded in the latter part of the seventeenth century, triggering feverish interest in Asian artistry. No less captivated than his people, the Sun King founded the *Compagnie des Indes Orientales* in 1664, intent upon endowing Versailles with Oriental lacquerware and porcelains. With the aristocracy wanting what they saw, the passion for Chinese symbols of status spread far beyond the court.

At first, only the ruling class could afford the porcelain vases, silk screens, and embroidered hangings, not to mention the lacquered cabinets with gleaming varnish finishes and hand-painted motifs, which commanded forbiddingly high prices. But then wealthy Europeans sought objects from exotic places, and demand soared. With the potential for an even more lucrative market for everything Oriental, *marchands-merciers* began importing a barrage of furnishings and decorative art, in hopes of selling to a wider audience.

When demand outstripped supply at the price points offered, the French, as well as other Europeans, introduced richly decorated pieces that liberally interpreted Oriental motifs and forms. The melding of Far Eastern inspiration and Western craftsmanship in the seventeenth century launched a style that would become known as *chinoiserie*. And demand further soared as pieces became more attainable.

Impatient for a respite from palace protocol, Louis XIV in 1670 ordered his architect, Louis Le Vau, to build the *Trianon de Porcelaine*—a group of five single-story pavilions—on the grounds of Versailles. When complete, the king decorated the structures in floor-to-ceiling chinoiserie. (The cluster was destroyed in 1687, presumably because neither the king's architect nor anyone else had the slightest notion what Chinese buildings looked like at the time, let alone knowledge of the woods and other materials indigenous to central and southern China used in construction. Another Trianon replaced it.)

Louis XV shared his great-grandfather's penchant for the luster and exoticism of chinoiserie, as did his mistress, Madame de Pompadour, who designed a *chambre a la torque* (Turkish bedroom) for herself at the Château de Bellevue, which was custom-built to her specifications.

It would be centuries, however, before French artisans could duplicate the exquisite reflective property of Chinese lacquer. Yet taking artistic license, they continued adding exuberant decorations of their own to the pagodas, blossoming trees, birds, dragons, and other motifs that motivated

them. As they moved away from the dense patterns that characterized early designs, playful monkeys garbed in Chinese costumes pranced across fabrics and wallcoverings, mimicking human behavior. (The motifs were called, appropriately enough, *singerie*—as in French, *singe* means "monkey.")

With neoclassical reaction against the rococo, the fashion for chinoiserie declined. Today, however, the demand for Chinese furnishings continues to swell. With supply limited, the finest pieces fetch record prices at American auction houses—giving rise in China to a cottage industry of runners who travel from village to village knocking on doors to buy black lacquered tables, walnut chairs, fanciful benches, and other artifacts. On both sides of the Atlantic, those captivated by Chinese flair knowingly include eighteenth-century chinoiserie furnishings in their homes.

THEATER

TICKETS

A World Away

Design-savvy parents raise the bar for a game room and in turn offer their children's circle of friends a fun-filled place to hang out. With the pomp befitting a much loved someone, a lighted marquee heralds a special day.

A World Away

The French shun most anything that hints of material excess or, for that matter, has potential for spawning envy. But Americans often take a different tack. For on this side of the Atlantic, there's no shame in making waves in *châteaux* buffed to look centuries old, wine cellars with tasting areas, and private theaters with wireless surround sound, anymore than with yachts that extend well over 150 feet, time-shares at elite resorts, or trips to the ancient cities of the Orient.

Powder room door.

Fortunately, in a country awash in luxury, it is fine to rise above it all with the out of the ordinary, particularly when accomplishments rather than high birth are the foundation of one's financial worth. This, after all, is the way America works. And it is not apt to change if it hasn't since political economist and social critic Thorstein Veblen (1857–1929) coined the famous phrase "conspicuous consumption" in 1899—which was long before a number of us began unabashedly embracing everything from appliances that address a specific task to *boiserie* from iconic *hôtels particuliers*, let alone separate guest houses or more square footage in the absence of any obvious need.

OPPOSITE: *A screening room with movie-star allure offers front-row seats amidst state-of-the-art equipment—all unseen.*

This is not to say we are smitten by plush, trophy interiors or just about "bling." And certainly it is not that we don't have concerns that are more pressing—such as family worries, the rising cost of education, and the threat of terrorism—anymore than we believe that another accoutrement will give purpose to our lives. But in the United States, long-standing tradition doesn't weigh us down, depriving us of our ability to acquire what we please. After all, the American Revolution didn't promise the *liberté, égalité,* and *fraternité* that the French Revolution hoped to deliver. However, the Bill of Rights gave us certain "unalienable" rights, including the freedom to point out intrinsic differences in attitudes.

So, without making too much of American and French distinctions, for the most part, we abandon thoughts of what something says to others and instead consider what it means to us, knowing that our passion for glamour in all its forms is what gives our homes pizzazz. Is it really such a big deal, then,

A powder room looks like it stepped out of an old movie palace, thanks to an artist's eye.

if we find it difficult to curb an appetite for big-name commercial-looking ranges such as Viking, Garland, Thermador, or Wolf that leap, above all others, at the chance to assert their stainless steel presence? Or lust after the latest glass-front refrigerator with satellite storage areas? We think not. Pricey as all are, they often cost less than European rivals—and tap into our more-than-occasional need to purchase American-made products. Besides, the expensive crème de la crème La Cornue range has long been a staple in French kitchens—and this hardly puts Gauls in an unflattering light.

Aside from function, what matters most to Americans is a look in keeping with personal visions and passions. With some studies suggesting the kitchen is the socializing spot of choice, is it any wonder that one of the French capital's more than 2,600 cafés can be the ideal model? This, of course, requires sifting through today's menu of options and carefully selecting a few key elements that are not only up to the task but also up to making the space feel warm, comfortable, and inviting to a crowd.

While some essentials with extravagant price tags may be out of the price zone we have in mind, the cost of others can affront our sensibilities. Regardless, neither money nor social standing offers any guarantee of style. It cannot be found doing a Google search, nor can it be procured at a Whole Foods Market, anymore than obtained dashing madly about Europe. But then, style, like beauty, is in the eye of the beholder.

No matter that ideas about beauty were far less complex when the French were our passports to good taste. Lately we have become dependent upon our own discerning preferences rather than adhering to the French point of view. We aren't drawn, for example, to threadbare rugs or antiques with big chunks missing. > 161

No trip to the theater is complete without a stop at the concession stand.

With refrigerators becoming the new fashion item, sleek stainless steel shelves make this the perfect choice for an active Houston family.

OPPOSITE: *Even in a teardown, ruin of a house, some things can be worth saving. Surprisingly, it was the refrigerator that was worthy of note.*

ABOVE: *To the dismay of the French, Americans have no qualms about turning antique armoires with distinctive beauty into homes for electronics—or in this case, billiard cue sticks—satisfying twenty-first-century needs.*

BELOW: *Across from the billiards table is a spot reserved for chess.*

OPPOSITE: *Queen Marie Antoinette added numerous billiard rooms to Versailles and to the Petit Trianon, her personal retreat.*

And with more than a modicum of respect for exquisitely made tapestries, we are opposed to using them to cover damp, crumbling walls. As for ormolu, long ago most began to loose its luster; and we prefer painted Louis pieces instead of those baroque.

Finessing French style to suit our tastes, we also soundly reject old appliances—both seen and heard—and most everything else that reeks of simpler times for upscale luxuries du jour, such as restaurant-style faucets, subway-tiled walls, countertops made of honed white marble streaked, of course, with gray veins, and ceilings with pressed-tin squares washed in pewter.

As this country indulges in an unparalleled home-improvement spree—totaling $126.1 billion in 2004, up 15 percent from 2001, according to Harvard University's Joint Center for Housing studies—it turns out that kitchen remodeling is favored over other rooms in the house, perhaps because it plays a big role in increasing a home's resale value. For a similar reason, bathroom remodels also are popular.

By American standards, kitchens in France are remarkably modest, thanks to everything from being more about cooking than socializing to resistance to change from the time when they were servants' domains to a culture—founded on understatement—that believes in living more frugally than Americans do. Given these, most all the staples of high-tech style are missing. Appliances sit in plain sight. There are no twenty-first-century computer centers where older children can do their homework, or even family-friendly islands that keep pre-schoolers practicing scissor skills nearby.

In a country long the uncontested capital of *haute cuisine*, fittingly enough, kitchens are planned with an eye to convenience. Lower cabinets with nickel knobs line the walls, while doors are noticeably missing >167

Using oils, Houston artist Allen Rodewald created a mural with the unpretentious charm of rural France.

In a girly bedroom that's a world unto itself—with spots of sleeping and playing—the versatile daybed doubles as a place for taking naps. Later it will offer an ideal spot for a friend to have sweet dreams during a slumber party.

OPPOSITE: *A boy's passion for sports inspires a collection that adds to his fun. Wallcovering is from Ralph Lauren.*

ABOVE: *Detail of chair.*

CENTER: *Artist Bella Pallik (1845–1908) studied at the academies in both Vienna and Munich. At the esteemed Paris exhibition, or* salon, *in 1890 she received honorable mention.*

BELOW: *The influence of the French moves from the kitchen on page 166 into the dining room, where an unexpected taste of Spain awaits the photographer and author on a Louis XV cherry refectory table. Family recipes for gazpacho and tortilla warrant applause. The French olive bread and cheeses are added treats.*

OPPOSITE: *A Louis XVI trumeau (overmantel with mirror and painted scene) takes center stage in a New Orleans living room that is an inviting mélange of walnut wood pieces, fine fabrics, and subtle tones pulled from the antique Oushak carpet. Throw pillows adorned with Scalamandré trim began life in the eighteenth century as an Aubusson. The chandelier is from the fabled Marché aux Puces de Saint-Ouen.*

from upper shelves, which groan with most everything but the kitchen sink. Vying for space are stacks of plates, pitchers, bowls, and platters blasé about gathering dust—though wineglasses often stand upside down, restaurant-style. Countertops serve as the homeland of *la batterie de cuisine.*

Unlike Americans, who tend to tuck clutter out of sight, the French prefer that cutting boards, *porte-couverts* (cutlery holders with knives that carve, chop, pare, peel, and dice), richly glazed *confit* pots, small appliances, and baskets for storing fresh bread share space with collections of tin molds: some for baking fancy tartes Tatin, some for chocolate making, and some to satisfy cravings for sorbet or ice cream. Meanwhile, windowsills parade mossy pots of sage, rosemary, chives, and basil.

There's no question that even the humblest kitchen can rightly boast of being incredibly efficient as multitasking copper pots and pans sway from *crémaillères* (pot racks) within easy reach. And though the French admiration for pot racks is contagious, we ultimately push the limits of upscale finery in hopes of landing a five-star rating.

Leaving nothing to chance, hardwood floors sweep uninterrupted from dining rooms into some stateside kitchens. Sleek black-and-white tile laid in a checkerboard pattern creates interest in others. Predictably, perhaps, many Americans take a more obvious approach: letting reclaimed, oversized squares or octagons of unglazed terra-cotta tile with the flavor of Provence, Burgundy, and the Loire Valley, where clay is plentiful, complete the look.

Primed, painted and glazed with old-world know-how, cabinets artfully aged exude a beauty that never fades, not even as the sun streams through doors at the far end of the kitchen.

In the sixteenth century, beautiful table and bed linens were an important part of a noblewoman's dowry. The yearning for fine linens spread from royal residences to châteaux to hôtels particuliers and pieds-à-terre. Whether detailed subtly or elaborately, linens from prestigious D. Porthault are a hallmark of well-appointed homes today.

Before closets were commonplace, armoires offered ample storage for a family's linens or clothes. This is not to say we have forgotten that they originally housed armor, hence the name.

Bedding from Leontine Linens, New Orleans, blanket a painted nineteenth-century bed in the style of Louis XVI. Above hangs an antique boiserie fragment. The toile wall sconce is from the Paris Flea Market. Rose Cummings silk taffeta stripe curtains add more than a bit of glamour to the guest room.

Marketers rejoice as our mulling over what to do leads to plunging into redesigning a bath or powder room, too. For, now, neither is considered a strictly functional place, as in earlier eras, when catering to the body's every whim might be thought self-absorbed. With research suggesting that we are lingering longer in the bathroom, it makes perfect sense that we take inspiration from the *salles de bain* in Paris's most luxurious hotels, where heated towel rails, gleaming fittings, and showerheads as large as the moon quiet the mind, soothe the senses, and befriend the spirit in satisfying doses.

At the capital's elegant Plaza Athénée Hôtel, as well as at the Hôtel de Crillon—where the Treaty of Paris recognizing the independence of the United States was signed on February 6, 1778—color is a rarity. (In Parisian minds, the feeling is that strong hues are not easy to live with for long.) Out of favor, too, is the built-in vanity, despite its considerable merits. Instead, white pedestal sinks with easily maintained nickel fittings or washstands with polished nickel legs, marble slab tops, and under-counter mounted porcelain basins compete for space. The beveled mirrors—in wide, classic frames—that accompany them give even small areas more presence. The French seldom affix mirrors to walls.

It follows that thick, gently scented bath sheets, hand towels, and wash mitts wait to be called into service. *Tissanes pour le bain*, or bath herbs in tiny cheesecloth sachets, and soap made from formulas often dating back centuries, further bathe one in luxury. But above all, natural light ranks near the top of priority lists.

For our part, a mix of luxury and the practical seduces us. Together they compel us to create posh interiors replete with warmth that bear no resemblance to Versailles. Focusing on what our visions say to others went out of fashion decades ago. Instead, what matters most these days is what works for the important people and pets in our lives—and us.

The master bedroom in New Orleans, the most Gallic of American cities, reminds us that in 1803, the United States more than doubled its size by buying an uncharted 828,000-square-mile territory from France for fifteen million dollars.

The Beauty of Versailles

Sculptress Corrine Hartley resides in Newport Beach, California.

The Beauty of Versailles

Centuries-old finials that originally adorned a building on the outskirts of Rome have a new home in the estates.

The French like to say that the beauty of Versailles flows in their blood, which is not hard to believe when tributes to the palace literally abound. No matter that the ever-so-lavish former home and glorious gardens of Louis XIV are not exactly known for understatement: both fit the Sun King's guiding vision as well as the extravagance of the time. And while one might suspect that the expression is at odds with the French public persona, this seems not to be the case. Quite to their liking, it highlights the deep cultural bond between the palace and the people, the result of ties born hundreds of years ago.

Yet with all due respect to the French, they are hardly the only ones genetically predisposed. Thanks to the 25,000 or so genes implanted deep in the genome, with each generation the enduring influence of Versailles travels far beyond the French Republic's borders. Each year an estimated three million admirers—some from within the country, but even more from outside it—wander through the magnificent château and then traverse its celebrated, meticulously planned grounds stretching across 1,700 acres. (Maison de la France, a travel trade organization keeping tabs, reports Americans are the largest contingent of foreign visitors to the country, totaling more than 4.5 million in 2001, the latest year for which figures are available.) Regardless that the seven-hundred-room château and its grounds are now undergoing a $450-million makeover expected to take two decades, many obsess over the Baroque perfection of architect Jules Hardouin Mansart's Hall of Mirrors.

A gazebo serves as a reminder of the magnificence of Versailles, where a Romanesque gazebo rises behind the Petit Trianon.

Meanwhile, serious gardeners take inspiration from Versailles's famous park, in particular. Walking leisurely along the curving paths, gazing approvingly at the sculptures, photographing in the morning light, those longing to improve their own environments set their sights on seizing a bit of the wonder. For the dignity of Versailles makes the challenging seem attainable a continent away.

From Savannah to San Francisco and St. Louis in between, the classical influence of Versailles is easy to spot as residents adhere to the same key principles: logic, order, discipline, and beauty. Whether land is rolling or flat, pea gravel paths separate well-defined patterns of squares and rectangles. Plantings sectioned geometrically into smaller beds captivatingly boast exacting mirror images. Statuary of mythological figures, graceful fountains, and shapely urns spilling over with foliage lend dimension to sculptured, manicured estates surely less formal than the Palace of Versailles at its lavish best.

In a testament to the park's varied beauty—carefully planned by the great landscape artist André Le Nôtre (1613–1700) more than three hundred years ago—savvy Americans borrow the principles he preached, published in *La Theorie et La Pratique du Jardinage* in 1739 by one of his pupils.

As it is, Le Nôtre's artistic concerns are as practical today as when they held sway in the seventeenth century. In short, he believed that aesthetic rewards come from a garden in harmony with the setting; planned with the climate in mind; in scale with the house; and, not least, fitting the needs and lifestyle of the owner, which was his way of saying in keeping with an ability to care properly for the land.

In creating his masterpieces, Le Nôtre laid the foundation for classical French gardens based on his conviction that man had the ability to dominate nature. Repeatedly employing the same standard plan, a château served as the design's central focus, with a central axis leading toward the structure, bisected by diverging paths. Each terrace, whether ascending or descending, helped create the optical illusion of infinite space without diminishing the size of the main house.

In 1861, Napoléon III ordered a building constructed in Paris to house indoor courts for Jeu de Paume, or "game of palm of the hand." The sport favored by French kings and played without rackets was the precursor to modern tennis. The historic structure, known as the Jeu de Paume, later housed Impressionist works of art—until French President François Mitterrand converted the Musée d'Orsay (a railroad station) into a museum in December 1986.

Born in Paris into a family of royal gardeners, André Le Nôtre was an obvious choice to succeed his father, Jean Le Nôtre, at the *Jardin des Tuileries* when the latter became head gardener to Louis XIII—just as Jean Le Nôtre had followed in his own father's footsteps at Tuileries Gardens, quite naturally, when summoned in 1592 to serve as landscaper to Queen Marie de Médici.

A gifted engineer with an artist's eye, André Le Nôtre set about in 1637 revamping the Tuileries—originally the city's garbage dump with clay soil used for making *tuiles* (tiles); hence its name. Before long, the regal avenue des Champs-Élysées would also bear his hallmark as he gave the broad boulevard even more presence by lacing it with parallel rows of chestnut trees and planting generous sweeps of brilliant-colored flowers.

In the meantime, he worked feverishly from 1656 to 1661 producing an extraordinary masterpiece for Nicholas Fouquet (1615–80), who served as minister of finance under Louis XIV. At Vaux-le-Vicomte, in rural Seine-et-Marne south of Paris, Le Nôtre redirected one of two rivers traversing the unspoiled terrain. Also, he carefully arranged a hierarchy of small spaces spawned from a central axis sweeping away from the grand château as far as the eye could see. Flower-banked reflecting pools, basins, and waterfalls, plus 1,200 fountains offered further proof of his imaginative hand.

Considering that everyone knew subjects were not to live more lavishly than the king, it may not have come as surprising news that Louis XIV sent for the artist responsible for the landscaping at Vaux-le-Vicomte and instructed him to exceed all prior triumphs at Versailles, where much of the land was a swamp. And indeed he did. Over the next thirty-three years, his laborers and he created extraordinary French gardens that were anything but minimal, laying out spacious terraces, *parterres* with winding pebble paths, and coppices, while turning marshes into imposing ornamental lakes, beautified with fountains and sculptures. Never mind that the decorative lakes necessitated funneling water via an aqueduct and network of pipes from the town of Marly (now Marly-le-Roi), roughly six kilometers away.

Fluted plates and bowls are from Bergdorf Goodman, New York.

Tree-lined forests, fruit groves, and impressive stone stairways traded on the king's desire for over-the-top extravagance, consciously or not. There were stately shrubs, sumptuous flower beds, and elaborate topiaries. Musical water fountains sprung to life, dancing in the air when the king approached; 460 are still working today. But perhaps most notably, Le Nôtre created a predilection for French gardens when most of the world was still enamored with Italian ones.

When André Le Nôtre died in 1700, France mourned the loss of the most famous landscape architect of the seventeenth century. Yet his unprecedented influence is still strongly felt as people from around the world continue taking their cues from his awe-inspiring designs at the sprawling Palace of Versailles.

OPPOSITE: *Whether morning, noon, or night, the terrace of the author's Colorado mountain home readily welcomes three generations of family fleeing the Texas heat. European-inspired nine-foot-diameter market umbrellas are from the Santa Barbara Collection for Giati Designs; furniture from Murray's Iron Works wear nature's hues.*

Inspired by a Houston family's love of entertaining, artist Jackie Haliburton—painted a gathering on the hood above the range in the loggia's fully equipped summer kitchen.

OPPOSITE: *A loggia open to the elements—as seen through the outdoor curtains—is more than an accessory to the house. With a fully equipped kitchen and array of notable amenities, including stylish seating from Murray's Iron Works, Los Angeles, it is perfect for entertaining en plein air.*

Garden Variety

Much as chic accessories bolster the power of any woman wearing Coco Chanel's (1883–1971) iconic *petit noir* (little black) dress, the French add cachet to their *maisons* from the outside in, believing that there is no better way to empower two disparate spaces than with a lavish dose of panache. For most, linking the house and garden is a matter of pride, with each space complementing rather than outshining the other, as harmonious extensions.

Masses of fresh flowers, handsome sisal rugs, caned *canapés* (settees), rush-seated chairs, and *bergères* with exposed hardwood frames give interiors a dose of sumptuous outdoor textures as daily life streams out early in the day. No matter that in much of the country, dining al fresco is only possible a few months a year, an abiding love for the land means that plantings may vary, but decorating from the outside in—and vice versa—is always in season. Much like the Impressionists, who were intent on capturing the effect of light on nature, here are a few of the many garden tools commonly used to enhance spaces *en plein air*:

Allée: A tree-lined walk, avenue, or wide path that brings grandeur to an entrance or frames a garden.

Arbor: *Tonnelle* in French. An outdoor room framed in latticework from which bougainvillea, wisteria, or other entwined climbing vines cascade, shading the setting.

Balustrade: A series of low, evenly spaced, vertical stone or concrete pillars topped by a rail that fashion a decorative enclosure for balconies, terraces, and stairways.

Belvédère: Italian for "beautiful view." A shelter sited on a rise of soil that takes advantage of the breeze and the view. It could be an open-sided pavilion, summerhouse, elaborate folie, or garden shed.

Bosquet: A carefully planned ornamental grove of trees—generally a single variety—pruned and planted in a formal grid and pierced by paths, thus creating an open-air drawing room. Sculptures and fountains stand among the trees at Versailles.

Bower: A shelter, akin to an arbor, shaped from entwined tree boughs or vines rather than supported by latticework.

Boxwoods: Various species of evergreen shrubs favored for hedges and topiaries in formal gardens, generally planted in orderly grids, then clipped and coaxed into geometric shapes such as domes or globes.

Broderie: French for "embroidery." Formal, embellished *parterres* (flower beds) bordered by tidy clipped hedges or pruned shrubs and pebble paths, forming an elaborate ornamental motif suggestive of embroidery.

Calades: River pebbles set into mortar in curving patterns, forming paths and terraces, particularly in Provence.

Calpinage: Bricks laid on edge, often in a herringbone pattern—commonly seen on paths and terraces in Provence.

Clair-voie: An opening in a garden wall, offering a clear view of the scenery on the opposite side.

Clôture vivante: French for "living fence," commonly created by weaving shrub branches together.

Courtyard: A cobblestone area behind imposing, heavily carved *hôtel particulier* doors where carriages stood waiting in the nineteenth century. Today, however, the building most likely houses separate living areas. And pale gravel or cobblestones offer a parking spot for cars in an open space surrounded by walls.

Cypress tree: A tree said to bring good fortune.

Espalier: Stems from medieval times when monks embellished garden walls with plantings trained to grow flat in sculptural patterns, but today more often refers to the practice of shaping tree branches and shrubs into stylized forms or training vines on wire to grow in a set direction to form a hedge.

Evergreens: Shrubs favored for hedges and topiaries. Evergreens are one of the most distinctive features of classical French gardens, since they can be enjoyed year-round.

Flowers: Until the nineteenth century, flowerbeds were not the focus of gardens. In fact, Louis XIV disliked flowers.

Gazebo: A freestanding, fanciful house open on all sides, often sited at the corner of a garden where it frequently stands sometimes two stories tall.

Grotte (feminine, grotto): A cave-like structure designed to provide a cool respite during warm weather.

Hedge: A dense row of shrubs that frames plantings or establishes the limits of a garden, much like a wall. Low hedges, such as boxwood, often section interior areas of a garden. Considered most formal are sheared yew, privet, and beech hedges.

Jardinière: An ornamental stand or container for flowers or plants, generally porcelain, that became popular in late eighteenth-century France.

Le jardin d'herbes: Herb garden.

Loggia: An open-sided shelter either freestanding or siding a house, suitable for use as an outdoor sitting room as well as for entertaining. A roof protects against the rain.

Parterre: French for "on the ground." A level garden bed—typically made up of flowers—with winding pebble paths geometrically dividing the plan.

Seventeenth-century Baroque textile patterns and hand-forged ironwork designs often copied the ornate, swirling patterns of parterres in France.

Parterre de broderie: An elaborate *parterre* whose flowering, plant-like designs resemble embroidery.

Path: A pebble walkway that divides planting beds and draws the eye to the farthest reaches.

Patte d'oie: The place where three, four, or five straight *allées*, or avenues, meet at sharp angles and form a shape similar to a goose's foot.

Pergola: An open-roofed structure fashioned with beams and cross members supported by a row of pillars or posts, from which flowers or plants cascade, creating a covered walkway.

Potager: A kitchen garden where vegetables and herbs are grown for mealtime consumption. Rooted in Italian gardens cultivated by monks and nuns, *potagers* supplied inhabitants of the abbeys with food and altars with flowers. At Versailles stands a statue of Jean-Baptiste de la Quintinie, Louis XIV's chief gardener and the creator of his ornamental kitchen garden.

Statuary: Likenesses of liberators and public symbols, as well as mythological figures and animals, important to French heritage.

Topiary: Trees and shrubbery fashioned into ornamental sculpted shapes. Sometimes set in large planters.

Treillage: Elaborate trelliswork, either freestanding or placed against a fence or wall, often designed to create depth and perspective.

Trellis: Any two-dimensional frame of latticework, whether attached to a wall or fence, or freestanding.

Tuteur: French for "stake." An ornamental freestanding trellis made of wood and obelisk in shape.

Urns: Symbolizing the abundance of the garden.

 Directory

Here is where to find the designers mentioned in this book.

Roberto G. Agnolini
Gerrold A. Powers
Bryan & Scott, Ltd.
112-114 North Tejon St.
Colorado Springs, CO 80903
Telephone: 719.633.9316

Bette Benton
Recollections
1005 South Shepherd St., Ste. 801
Houston, TX 77019
Telephone: 713.521.3531

David Corley, ASID
Julie Stryker
David Corley Interior Design
909 Dragon St.
Dallas, TX 75207
Telephone: 214.742.6767

Vicki Crew, Allied Member ASID
Vicki Crew Interior Design
4313 Edmondson Ave.
Dallas, TX 75205
Telephone: 214.522.3914

Sherry Hayslip, ASID and IIDA
Bree Hyatt
Hayslip Design Associates
2604 Fairmount St.
Dallas, TX 75201
Telephone: 214.871.9106

Karin Lanham
Karin's Interiors
117 Beaver Creek Plaza
Beaver Creek, CO 81620
Telephone: 970.949.5628

Heidi Ledoux
Ledoux Design Associates
4115 Blackhawk Plaza Cr., Ste. 100
Danville, CA 94506
Telephone: 925.964.0060

Lucy D. Ledoux, Allied Member ASID
Ledoux Design Associates
9627 Clos du Lac Cr.
Loomis, CA 95650
Telephone: 916.660.0600

Holly Heath Lydick
H. H. Lydick Interiors
2117 Mount Royal Terr.
Fort Worth, TX 76107
Telephone: 817.737.9626

Tammy Michaelis, ASID
Design Endeavors
227 Mill Trail Cr.
Sugar Land, TX 77478
Telephone: 281.242.8762

Roberta Peters
Roberta Peters Design
172 Centre St.
Mountain View, CA 94041
Telephone: 650.960.0512

Betty Lou Phillips, ASID
Interiors by BLP
4278 Bordeaux Ave.
Dallas, TX 75205
Telephone: 214.599.0191

Marilyn Phillips
Loren Interiors
1125 Riverbend Rd.
Houston, TX 77063
Telephone: 713.973.6475

Alix Rico
Design Source
419 Fairway Dr.
New Orleans, LA 70124
Telephone 504.488.0205

Aline Steinbach
Camille en Provence
Hameau de Lumières
Goult, France 84220
Téléphone: 0033.490.723.545

Chris Van Wyk
Chris Van Wyk Designs
75 Westover Terr.
Fort Worth, TX 76107
Telephone: 817.735.9400

Deborah Walker, ASID
Andrea Smith
Deborah Walker & Associates
1925 Cedar Springs Rd., Ste. 103
Dallas, TX 75201
Telephone: 214.521.9637

DIRECTORY OF ARCHITECTS

Richard Drummond Davis **Richard Drummond Davis Architect**
4310 Westside Dr., Ste. H
Dallas, TX 75209
Telephone: 214.521.8763
www.rddavisarchitect.com

Cole Smith, FAIA
Dean W. Smith, AIA and CSI
Smith, Ekblad & Associates, Inc.
2719 Laclede St.
Dallas, Texas 75204
Telephone: 214.871.0305

DESIGNER AND ARCHITECT PHOTOGRAPHIC CREDITS

Roberto G. Agnolini: 140, 141, 142, 143, 144, 145

Bette Benton: 130, 131, 132, 133, 134, 135, 136, 137

David Corley and Julie Stryker: 58–59, 60, 62, 63

Vicki Crew:20, 21, 22, 23

Richard Drummond Davis, Architect: 12–13, 14, 15, 17, 18

PHOTOGRAPHER CREDITS

A morning room off the kitchen sends a kind invitation to savor a café au lait à deaux *and discuss world issues. Antique tapestry fragments are now plump pillows, adorning a Cameron Collection sofa.*

OPPOSITE: *No matter that the ottoman of today is only vaguely reminiscent of the long backless settee from which the privileged sultan of the vast Ottoman Empire ruled during the fourteenth century. From an ottoman, Jackson, the author's Norwich terrier rules.*

Exposed beams and copper pots garnish a country kitchen stocked with cabinets sporting a hammered design. Honed stone countertops flaunt irregular seams.

Resources

ANTIQUE FURNISHINGS

Agostino Antiques, Ltd.
21 Broad. St.
Red Bank, NJ 07701
Telephone 732.345.7301
www.agostinoantiques.com

Ambiance Antiques
135 Rhode Island St.
San Francisco, CA 94103
Telephone 415.255.9006
www.ambianceantiques.com

Annette Schatte Antiques
1928 Bissonnet St.
Houston, TX 77005
Telephone 713.524.0990

Artisan Imports
90 Safe Trek Pl., Ste. C
Bozeman, MT 59718
Telephone 406.585.7273
www.artisanimports.com

B. Bourgeois Antiques
270 Main St. South
Woodbury, CT 06798
Telephone 203.263.7770
www.bbourgeoisantiques.com

Bremermann Designs
3943 Magazine St.
New Orleans, LA 70115
Telephone 504.891.7763
www.bremermanndesigns.com

Brian Stringer Antiques
2031 West Alabama St.
Houston, TX 77006
Telephone 713.526.7380

Burden & Izett, Ltd.
180 Duane St.
New York, NY 10013
Telephone 212.941.8247
www.burdenandizett.net

Carl Moore Antiques
1610 Bissonnet St.
Houston, TX 77005
Telephone 713.524.2502
www.carlmooreantiques.com

Charles Gaylord Antiques
2151 Powell St.
San Francisco, CA 94133
Telephone 415.392.6085

Château Dominque
3615-B West Alabama St.
Houston, TX 77027
Telephone 713.961.3444
www.chateaudomingue.com

Country French Interiors
1428 Slocum St.
Dallas, TX 75207
Telephone 214.747.4700
www.countryfrenchinteriors.com

Décor de France
24 North Blvd. of the Presidents
Sarasota, FL 34236
Telephone 941.388.1599
www.decordefrance.com

Duane Antiques
176 Duane St.
New York, NY 10013
Telephone 212.625.8066
www.duaneantiques.com

Ed Hardy San Francisco
188 Henry Adams St.
San Francisco, CA 94103
Telephone 415.626.6300
www.edhardysf.com

The French Attic
71 Westbrook Dr., RR # 3
Komoka, Ontario
NOL 1 RO Canada
Telephone 519.319.6034
www.french-attic.com

The French Hare, Ltd.
418 King St.
Charleston, SC 29403
Telephone 843.577.0451
www.thefrenchhare.com

French Influences
49 Bennett St.
Atlanta, GA 30309
Telephone 404.367.4425

The Gables
711 Miami Cr.
Atlanta, GA 30324
Telephone 800.753.3342
www.thegablesantiques.com

Galerie de France
184-186 Duane St.
New York, NY 10013
Telephone 212.965.0969

Gore Dean Antiques
2828 Pennsylvania Ave.
Washington, DC 20007
Telephone 202.625.1776
www.goredeanantiques.com

A dining room in Colorado gets a welcome dose of warmth. Eighteenth-century chairs touting cut velvet once graced an opera house in Lyon. From the same era is the dining table of Spanish descent.

The Gray Door
1809 West Gray St.
Houston, TX 77019
Telephone 713.521.9085

Habité Antiques
963 Harrison St.
San Francisco, CA 94107
Telephone 415.543.3515
www.habite.com

Hideaway House
143 North Robertson Blvd.
Los Angeles, CA 90048
Telephone 310.276.4319
www.hideawayhouse.com

Inessa Stewart Antiques
5330 Bluebonnet Blvd.
Baton Rouge, LA 70809
Telephone 225.368.8600
www.inessa.com

Inessa Stewart Antiques
5201 West Lovers Ln.
Dallas, TX 75209
Telephone 214.366.2660
www.inessa.com

Jacqueline Adams
2300 Peachtree Rd.
Atlanta, GA 30309
Telephone 404.355.8123
www.jacquelineadamsantiques.com

Jacqueline Adams Antiques
425 Peachtree Hills Ave.
Atlanta, GA 30305
Telephone 404.869.6790
www.jacquelineadamsantiques.com

Jane Moore Interiors
2922 Virginia St.
Houston, TX 77098
Telephone 713.526.6113

John Rosselli & Associates
255 East 72nd St.
New York, NY 100121
Telephone 212.737.2252

John Rosselli & Associates
523 East 73rd St.
New York, NY 10021
Telephone 212.772.2137

Joseph Minton Antiques
1410 Slocum St.
Dallas, TX 75207
Telephone 214.744.3111
www.mintonantiques.com

Joyce Horn Antiques
1008 Wirt Rd.
Houston, TX 77055
Telephone 713.688.0507

Le Louvre French Antiques
1313 Slocum St.
Dallas, TX 75207
Telephone 214.742.2605
www.lelouvre-antiques.com

Lee Stanton Antiques
769 North La Cienega Blvd.
Los Angeles, CA 90069
Telephone 310.855.9800
www.leestanton.com

Lee Stanton Antiques
31531 Camino Capistrano
San Juan Capistrano, CA 92675
Telephone: 949.240.5181
www.leestanton.com

Legacy Antiques
1406 Slocum St.
Dallas, TX 75207
Telephone 214.748.4606
www.legacyantiques.com

The Lotus Collection
445 Jackson St.
San Francisco, CA 94111
Telephone 415.398.8115
www.ktaylor-lotus.com

Lovers Lane Antique Market
5001 West Lovers Ln.
Dallas, TX 75209
Telephone 214.351.5656
www.loversLn.antiques.com

Made In France
2912 Ferndale St.
Houston, TX 77098
Telephone 713.529.7949

Maison Felice
73-960 El Paseo
Palm Desert, CA 92260
Telephone 760.862.0021
www.maisonfelice.com

Marston Luce
1651 Wisconsin Ave., N.W.
Washington, DC 20007
Telephone 202.333.6800

Metropolitan Artifacts, Inc.
4783 Peachtree Rd.
Atlanta, GA 30341
Telephone 770.986.0007
www.metropolitanartifacts.com

The Mews
1708 Market Center Blvd.
Dallas, TX 75207
Telephone 214.748.9070
www.themews.net

Newell Art Galleries, Inc.
425 East 53rd St.
New York, NY 10022
Telephone 212.758.1970
www.newel.com

Niall Smith
306 East 61st St.
New York, NY 10021
Telephone 212.750.3985

Nick Brock Antiques
2909 North Henderson St.
Dallas, TX 75206
Telephone 214.828.0624

Orion Antique Importers, Inc.
1435 Slocum St.
Dallas, TX 75207
Telephone 214.748.1177
www.oriondallas.com

Pittet & Co.
1215 Slocum St.
Dallas, TX 75207
Telephone 214.748.8999
www.pittet.com

Shabby Slip
3522 Magazine St.
New Orleans, LA 70115
Telephone 504.897.5477

Sidney Lerer
420 Richmond Ave.
Point Pleasant Beach, NJ 08741
Telephone 732.899.8949

South of Market
345 Peachtree Hills Ave.
Atlanta, GA 30305
Telephone 404.995.9399
www.southofmarket.biz

Therien Studio Workshops.
716 North La Cienega Blvd.
Los Angeles, CA 90069
Telephone 310.657.4615
www.therien.com

Vieux Carré
546 Hudson St.
New York, NY 10014
Telephone 212.647.7633

The Whimsey Shoppe Slocum
1444 Oak Lawn Ave.
Dallas, TX 75207
Telephone 214.745.1800

Uncommon Market, Inc.
2701-2707 Fairmount St.
Dallas, TX 75201
Telephone 214.871.2775

Watkins, Culver, Gardner
2308 Bissonnet St.
Houston, TX 77005
Telephone 713.529.0597

Tres Belle
2435 East Coast Hwy.
Corona Del Mar, CA 92625
Telephone 949.723.0022

Fort Worth designer Chris Van Wyk framed the windows in a richly woven Scalamandré wool paisley, and then lined the curtains in a faux leather, as protection from the strong sun.

ARTISANS

Jennifer Chapman
Jennifer Chapman Designs
7049 Via Cabana
Carlsbad, CA 92009
Telephone 760.602.0079
www.jenniferchapmandesign.com

Manuel Cruz
1020 Andrews Dr.
Martinez, CA 94553
Telephone 925 370 7774
www.manuelcruz.com

Kay Fox's Custom Creations
2404 Springpark Way
Richardson, TX 75082
Telephone 972-437-4227

David Lyles
514 Summit Dr.
Richardson, TX 75081
Telephone 972.240.0051
www.seedavidlyles.com

Allan Rodewald
1402 Dart Ave.
Houston, TX 77007
Telephone 713.222.7443
www.alanrodewald.com

BATH FITTINGS

Czech & Speake
350 11th St.
Hoboken, NJ 07030
Telephone 800.632.4165
www.homeportfolio.com

Herbeau Creations of America
2725 Davis Blvd.
Naples, FL 34104
Telephone 800.547.1608
www.herbeau.com

Kallista, Inc.
2446 Verna Court
San Leandro, CA 94577
Telephone 888.4.Kallista
www.kallistainc.com

Sherle Wagner, International
60 East 57th St.
New York, NY 10022
Telephone 212.758.3300
www.sherlewagner.com

Sunrise Specialty
930 98th Ave.
Oakland, CA 94603
Telephone 510.729.7277
www.sunrisespecialty.com

Waterworks
60 Backus Ave.
Danbury, CT 06810
Telephone 800.899.6757
www.waterworks.com

CARPETS

Asmara, Inc.
88 Black Falcon Ave.
Boston, MA 02210
Telephone 800.451.7240
www.asmarainc.com

Beauvais Carpets
201 East 57th St.
New York, NY 10022
Telephone 212.688.2265
www.beauvaiscarpets.com

Carol Piper Rugs, Inc.
1809 West Gray St.
Houston, TX 77019
Telephone 713.524.2442
www.carolpiperrugs.com

Design Materials
241 South 55th St.
Kansas City, KA 66106
Telephone 913.342.9796

Mark, Inc.
323 Railroad Ave.
Greenwich, CT 06830
Telephone 203.861.0110
www.brunschwig.com

Nouri & Sons Antique Oriental
Rugs
3845 Dunlavy St.
Houston, TX 77006
Telephone 713.523.6626
www.nouriantiquerugs.com

Renaissance Collection
1532 Hi Line Dr.
Dallas, TX 75207
Telephone 214.698.1000
www.rencollection.com

Rosecore Carpet Co., Inc.
D&D Building
979 Third Ave.
New York, NY 10022
Telephone 212.421.7272
www.rosecore.com

Stark Carpet
D&D Building
979 Third Ave.
New York, NY 10022
Telephone 212.752.9000
www.starkcarpet.com

Stephen Miller Gallery
800 Santa Cruz Ave.
Menlo Park, CA 94025
Telephone 650.327.5040
www.stephenmillergallery.com

FABRICS / WALLCOVERINGS

Beaumont & Fletcher
F. Schumacher & Co.
1025 North Stemmons Freeway
Dallas, TX 75207
Telephone 214.748.3331
www.beaumontandfletcher.com

Bennison Fabrics
76 Greene St.
New York, NY 10012
Telephone 212.941.1212
www.bennisonfabrics.com

Bergamo Fabrics
7 West 22nd St., 2nd Fl.
New York, NY 10011
Telephone 212.462.1010
www.bergamofabrics.com

Boussac Fadini
15 East 32nd St., 6th Fl.
New York, NY 10016
Telephone 212.213.3099

Brunschwig & Fils, Inc.
75 Virginia Rd.
North White Plains, NY 10603
Telephone 914.684.5800
www.brunschwig.com

French and Italian architectural treasures at Château Dominque, Houston, await new homes in the States.

Carlton V
D&D Building
979 Third Ave., 15th Fl.
New York, NY 10022
Telephone 212.355.4525

Christopher Norman Inc.
41 West 25th St., 10th Fl.
New York, NY 10010
Telephone 212.647.0303
www.christophernorman.com

Clarence House
211 East 58th St.
New York, NY 10022
Telephone 212.752.2890
www.clarencehouse.com

Coraggio Textiles
1750 132nd Ave., N.E.
Bellevue, WA 98005
Telephone 425.462.0035
www.coraggio.com

Cowtan & Tout
111 Eighth Ave., Ste. 930
New York, NY 10011
Telephone 212.647.6900

Florio Collection
8815 Dorrington Ave.
West Hollywood, CA 90048
Telephone 310.273.8003
www.floriocollection.com

Fortuny, Inc.
D&D Building
979 Third Ave., 16th Fl.
New York, NY 10022
Telephone 212.753.7153
www.fortunyonline.com

Henry Calvin Fabrics
2046 Lars Way
Medford, OR 97501
Telephone 541.732.1996
www.henrycalvin.com

Jim Thompson
1694 Chantilly Dr.
Atlanta, GA 30324
Telephone 800.262.0336
www.jimthompson.com

Lee Jofa
225 Central Ave. South
Bethpage, NY 11714
Telephone 888.LeeJofa
www.leejofa.com

Marvic Textiles
30-10 41st Ave., 2nd Fl.
Long Island City, NY 11101
Telephone 718.472.9715

Nancy Corzine
256 West Ivy Ave.
Inglewood, CA 90302
Telephone 310.672.6775

Nobilis
57-A Industrial Rd.
Berkeley Heights, NJ 07922
Telephone 800.464.6670
www.nobilis.fr

Old World Weavers
D&D Building
979 Third Ave., 10th Fl.
New York, NY 10022
Telephone 212.355.7186
www.old-world-weavers.com

Osborne & Little
90 Commerce Rd.
Stamford, CT 06902
Telephone 203.359.1500
www.osborneandlittle.com

Pierre Frey, Ltd.
12 East 32nd St.
New York, NY 10016
Telephone 212.213.3099

RJF International Corp.
3875 Embassy Parkway
Fairlawn, OH 44333
Telephone 330.668.7600
www.sanitaswallcoverings.com

Roger Arlington, Inc.
30-10 41st Ave., Ste. 2R
Long Island City, NY 11101
Telephone 718.729.5554

Rogers & Goffigon Ltd.
41 Chestnut St., Ste. 3
Greenwich, CT 06830
Telephone 203.532.8068

Rose Cumming
Fine Arts Building
232 East 59th St., 5th Fl.
New York, NY 10022
Telephone 212.758.0844
www.rosecumming.com

Scalamandré
300 Trade Zone Dr.
Ronkonkoma, NY 11779
Telephone 631.467.8800
www.scalamandre.com

F. Schumacher Company
79 Madison Ave., 14th Fl.
New York, NY 10016
Telephone 212.213.7900
www.fschumacher.com

Silk Trading Co.
360 South La Brea Ave.
Los Angeles, CA 90036
Telephone 323.954.9280
www.silktrading.com

Travers
504 East 74th St.
New York, NY 10021
Telephone 212.772.2778
www.traversinc.com

FURNITURE

Cameron Collection
150 Dallas Design Center
1025 North Stemmons Freeway
Dallas, TX 75207
Telephone 214.744.1544

Dennis & Leen
8734 Melrose Ave.
Los Angeles, CA 90069
Telephone 310.652.0855

The Farmhouse Collection, Inc.
807 Russet St.
Twin Falls, ID 83301
Telephone 208.736.8700
www.farmhousecollection.com

Hamilton, Inc.
8417 Melrose Pl.
Los Angeles, CA 90069
Telephone 323.655.9193

Niermann Weeks
Fine Arts Building
232 East 59th St.
New York, NY 10022
Telephone 212.319.7979
www.niermannweeks.com

Patina, Inc.
351 Peachtree Hills Ave., N.E.
Atlanta, GA 30304
Telephone 800.635.4365
www.patinainc.com

Reynière Workshop
142 Oak Rd.
Monroe, NY 10950
Telephone 845.774.1541

Rose Tarlow/Melrose House
8454 Melrose Pl.
Los Angeles, CA 90069
Telephone 323.653.2122
www.rosetarlow.com

Shannon & Jeal
722 Steiner St.
San Francisco, CA 94117
Telephone 415.563.2727
www.s-j.com

Summer Hill, Ltd
2682 Middlefield Rd.
Redwood City, CA 94063
Telephone 650.363.2600
www.summerhill.com

INTERIOR ORNAMENTATION

J. P. Weaver
941 Air Way
Glendale, CA 91201
Telephone 818.500.1740
www.jpweaver.com

IRON WORK

Brun Metal Crafts, Inc.
2791 Industrial Ln.
Bloomfield, CO 80020
Telephone 303.466.2513

Cole Smith, FAIA and ASID
Smith, Ekblad & Associates
2719 Laclede St.
Dallas, TX 75204
Telephone 214.871.0305

Ironies
2222 Fifth St.
Berkeley, CA 94710
Telephone 510.644.2100

Murray's Iron Work
5915 Blackwelder St.
Culver City, CA 90232
Telephone 866.649.4766

Potter Art Metal
4500 North Central Expwy.
Dallas, TX 75206
Telephone 214.821.1419.
www.potterartmetal.com

LINENS

Frette
799 Madison Ave.
New York, NY 10021
Telephone 212.988.5221

Peacock Alley
4311 Oak Lawn Ave., Ste. 150
Dallas, TX 75219
Telephone 214.520.6736
www.peacockkalley.com

D. Porthault, Inc.
18 East 69th St.
New York, NY 10021
Telephone 212.688.1660
www.d-porthault.com

Pratesi
829 Madison Ave.
New York, NY 10021
Telephone 212.288.2315
www.pratesi.com

Yves Delorme
1725 Broadway Ave.
Charlottesville, VA 22902
Telephone 800.322.3911
www.yvesdelorme.com

LIGHTING, LAMPS, AND CUSTOM LAMP SHADES

Ann Morris Antiques
239 East 60th St.
New York, NY 10022
Telephone 212.755.3308

Chameleon
231 Lafayette St.
New York, NY 10012
Telephone 212.343.9197

Marvin Alexander, Inc.
315 East 62nd St., 2nd Fl.
New York, NY 10021
Telephone 212.838.2320

Murray's Iron Work
5915 Blackwelder St.
Culver City, CA 90232
Telephone 310.839.7737

Nesle
151 E 57th St.
New York, NY 10022
Telephone 212.755.0515
www.dir-dd.com/nesle.html

Niermann Weeks
Fine Arts Building
232 East 59th St., 1st Fl.
New York, NY 10022
Telephone 212.319.7979

Panache
719 North La Cienega Blvd.
Los Angeles, CA 90069
Telephone 310.652.5050

Vaughan Designs, Inc.
979 Third Ave., Ste. 1511
New York, NY 10022
Telephone 212.319.7070
www.vaughandesigns.com

STONE AND TILE

Ann Sacks Tile & Stone Inc.
8120 N.E. 33rd Dr.
Portland, OR 97211
Telephone 800.278.8453
www.annsacks.com

Country Floors
15 East 16th St.
New York, NY 10003
Telephone 212.627.8300
www.countryfloors.com

Paris Ceramics
151 Greenwich Ave.
Greenwich, CT 06830
Telephone 888.845.3487
www.parisceramics.com

Renaissance Tile & Bath
349 Peachtree Hills Ave., N.E.
Atlanta, GA 30305
Telephone 800.275.1822

Roof Tile & Slate Company
1209 Carroll St.
Carrollton, TX 75006
Telephone 972.242.7785
www.claytile.com

Tesserae Mosaic Studio, Inc.
1111 North Jupiter, Ste. 108A
Plano, TX 75074
Telephone 972-578-9006
www.tesseraemosaicstudio.com

Walker Zanger
8901 Bradley Ave.
Sun Valley, CA 91352
Telephone 877.611.0199
www.walkerzanger.com

TRIMMINGS AND PASSEMENTERIE

Houlès USA Inc.
8584 Melrose Ave.
Los Angeles, CA 90069
Telephone 310.652.6171
www.houles.com

Kenneth Meyer Company
300 Kansas St., Ste. 104
San Francisco, CA 94103
Telephone 415.861.0118

Le Potager
108 West Brookdale Pl.
Fullerton, CA 92832
Telephone 714.680.8864

Leslie Hannon Custom Trimmings
4018 East 5th St.
Long Beach, CA 90814
Telephone 562.433.0161

Renaissance Ribbons
PO Box 699
Oregon House, CA 95961
Telephone 530.692.0842.
www.renaissanceribbons.com

Tassels & Trims
232 East 59th St.
New York, NY 10022
Telephone 212.754.6000

West Coast Trimming
7100 Wilson Ave.
Los Angeles, CA 90001
Telephone 323.587.0701

Iron work crowns a rotunda in the entry. Chandelier is custom.